IFRS ACCOUNTING MANUAL FOR SMALL AND MEDIUM BUSINESSES

A PRACTICAL IFRS ACCOUNTING GUIDE FOR NON-QUOTED COMPANIES

REVISED EDITION

By

Etim O. Uso

IFRS ACCOUNTING MANUAL FOR SMALL AND MEDIUM BUSINESSES

Copyright © 2015 Etim O. Uso.

All rights reserved. Reproduction of this publication either in part or whole; rendering, implementing, or enacting the solutions algorithm, design, or model used in this book as a software solution, motion picture, flow chart, etc. through any medium using any system architecture or platform without prior written permission of the author is prohibited. Furthermore, dissemination or distribution of any such material or product whether for profit, gain, or otherwise without the written permission of the author or the publisher is prohibited.

Cover photo credit: Canva

TABLE OF CONTENTS

TABLE OF CONTENTS	**III**
PREFACE	**1**
ELEMENT AND FUNDAMENTAL PRINCIPLES OF ACCOUNTING	**7**
WHAT IS ACCOUNTING?	7
ACCOUNTING METHODS	8
CLASSIFICATION	9
MEASUREMENTS	9
RECOGNITION	9
PRESENTATION	10
WHY ACCOUNTING?	10
ELEMENTS OF FINANCIAL STATEMENTS	11
ASSET	11
LIABILITY	12
EQUITY	12
INCOME	13
THE DIFFERENCE BETWEEN INCOME AND REVENUE	13
EXPENSE	14
UNDERSTANDING DEBIT AND CREDIT	15
THE FUNDAMENTAL LAW AND PRINCIPLES OF ACCOUNTING	16
THE LAW OF DOUBLE-ENTRY	17
HOW DOUBLE-ENTRY RESONATES WITH THE NATURAL LAWS...	18

PRACTICAL EXAMPLES WITH DOUBLE-ENTRY POSTINGS	19
KEY ASSUMPTIONS IN ACCOUNTING	**23**
ACCRUAL BASIS	23
GOING CONCERN	24

THE INTERNATIONAL FINANCIAL REPORTING STANDARDS (IFRS)   25

THE STANDARDS	**26**
IASB'S OBJECTIVE	**27**
FIRST-TIME ADOPTION OF THE IFRS	**28**
SPECIFIC IFRS REQUIREMENTS FOR FIRST-TIME ADOPTER	28
IFRS COMPLIANCE REQUIREMENTS	29
IFRS FOR SMEs	**31**
WHAT IS SME?	31
WHY IFRS FOR SMES?	32

THE BOOKS OF ACCOUNTS   35

THE BOOKS OF ACCOUNTS	**35**
THE JOURNAL	36
CASHBOOK	37
ACCOUNTS RECEIVABLE	37
ACCOUNTS PAYABLE	37
INVENTORY	37
FIXED ASSETS	37
COMPUTER-BASED ACCOUNTING SYSTEM	**38**

THE CHART OF ACCOUNTS   41

ACCOUNTS CODING CONVENTION	**43**

SAMPLE CHART OF ACCOUNTS   44

RECOGNITION AND MEASUREMENT OF REVENUE (AND EXPENSE)   51

RECOGNITION OF REVENUE   52
RECOGNITION OF REVENUE—SALE OF GOODS   52
RENDERING OF SERVICES   53
INTERESTS, ROYALTIES AND DIVIDENDS   54

TIMING FOR RECOGNITION OF REVENUE & EXPENSE   54
EARNED INCOME   55
UNEARNED (DEFERRED) INCOME   55
EXPENSE INCURRED   56
PREPAID EXPENSE   56
ACCRUED EXPENSE   57

WORKED EXAMPLES ON REVENUE AND EXPENSE RECOGNITION   58
RENDERING OF SERVICE   58
SALE OF GOODS   60

CUSTOMER LOYALTY PROGRAMME   63

THE PARADOX OF ACCRUED EXPENSE   64

CONSTRUCTION CONTRACTS   67

WHAT IS A CONSTRUCTION CONTRACT?   67

CONTRACT REVENUE AND COST   68

DETERMINATION OF PERCENTAGE OF COMPLETION   71

CONTRACT WORK IN PROGRESS   72

DISCLOSURE   73

INVENTORIES — 75

BASIC DEFINITIONS AND RECOGNITION OF INVENTORY — 75
- WHAT IS INVENTORY? — 75
- INVENTORY COST — 76
- NET REALIZABLE VALUE (NRV) — 76

MEASUREMENT OF INVENTORY COST — 76
- INVENTORY COSTS AND COSTING METHODS — 77
- INVENTORIES WRITE-DOWN — 77

STANDARD ACCOUNTING ENTRIES ASSOCIATED WITH INVENTORY — 78
- SALES — 78
- PURCHASES — 79
- WRITE-DOWN — 79
- WRITE-DOWN REVERSAL — 79
- TRANSFERS — 79
- MANUAL INVENTORY UPDATES — 80

THE INVENTORY REGISTER — 80

ACCOUNTING FOR SALARY & WAGES — 83

PAYROLL ACCOUNTING METHODS — 84
- ACCOUNTING FOR EARNINGS — 85
- ACCOUNTING FOR DEDUCTIONS — 85
- PREPARING AND PAYING SALARY — 87
- ACCRUED SALARY — 88

SUMMARY OF ACCOUNTS REQUIRED FOR PAYROLL — 89

TAXES — 91
- TYPES OF TAXES — 91
- GENERAL ACCOUNTING ENTRIES FOR TAX — 92

ACCOUNTING FOR WITHHOLDING TAX — 93

ACCOUNTING ENTRIES FOR WITHHOLDING TAX	94
ACCOUNTING FOR VALUE-ADDED TAX (VAT)	**95**
CLASSIFICATION OF VALUE-ADDED TAX	96
ACCOUNTING ENTRIES FOR VALUE-ADDED TAX	96

PROPERTY, PLANT AND EQUIPMENT (FIXED ASSETS) 101

DEFINITION AND RECOGNITION CRITERIA	**102**
ASSET COST	102
USEFUL LIFE	103
RESIDUAL VALUE	103
DEPRECIABLE AMOUNT	103
DEPRECIATION	104
CARRYING AMOUNT	104
FAIR VALUE	105
RECOVERABLE AMOUNT	105
IMPAIRMENT	105
MEASUREMENTS POLICY	**105**
INITIAL MEASUREMENT	105
SUBSEQUENT MEASUREMENTS	106
COMPONENTIZATION	107
CHANGES IN ESTIMATES	108
IMPAIRMENTS	108
COMPONENT REPLACEMENT OR UPGRADE	108
DE-RECOGNITION	**110**
SALE	111
WRITE-OFF	111
TRANSFER	113
IMPLEMENTATION ISSUES	**113**
CLASSIFICATION	114
SELECTION OF ACCOUNTING POLICIES	114
BUILDING THE FIXED ASSETS REGISTER	114
APPLYING THE POLICIES	115

DISCLOSURES	115
SIMPLIFICATIONS FOR SMES	**116**

LEASES   117

DEFINITIONS & RECOGNITION	**117**
WHAT IS A LEASE?	117
INCEPTION OF A LEASE	117
RECOGNITION OF A LEASE	118
CLASSIFICATION OF LEASES	118
LEASE INVOLVING LAND AND BUILDING	118
LEASE MEASUREMENTS FOR *LESSEES*	**119**
FINANCE LEASE	119
OPERATING LEASES	120
LEASE MEASUREMENTS FOR *LESSOR*	**120**
FINANCE LEASE MEASUREMENTS	120
OPERATING LEASE MEASUREMENTS	121
SUMMARY OF ACCOUNTING ENTRIES FOR LEASES	**122**
FINANCE LEASE	122
OPERATING LEASE	124

FINANCIAL STATEMENTS AND SUNDRY REPORTS   127

FINANCIAL STATEMENTS	**128**
A COMPLETE SET OF FINANCIAL STATEMENTS	128
IDENTIFICATION AND PRESENTATION OF THE FINANCIAL STATEMENTS	128
STATEMENT OF FINANCIAL POSITION	129
STATEMENT OF COMPREHENSIVE INCOME (INCOME STATEMENT)	130
OTHER COMPREHENSIVE INCOME (OCI)	131
TOTAL COMPREHENSIVE INCOME	132
STATEMENT OF CHANGES IN EQUITY	133
STATEMENT OF CASH FLOWS	134

GENERAL DISCLOSURES REQUIREMENTS	134
CUSTOM FINANCIAL REPORTS	**135**

STATEMENT OF CASH FLOWS — 137

UNDERSTANDING CASH FLOWS	**137**
CLASSIFICATION OF CASH FLOW	**139**
CASH FROM OPERATING ACTIVITIES	139
CASH FROM INVESTING ACTIVITIES	139
CASH FROM FINANCING ACTIVITIES	139
HOW TO CALCULATE CASH FLOW	**140**
NET PROFIT	140
DEPRECIATION EXPENSE	140
ASSET	140
LIABILITY	141
DISCLOSURE REQUIREMENTS	**142**

CLOSING THE BOOKS — 143

CLOSING AND OPENING BALANCES	**143**

ACCOUNTING AND THE INFORMATION SYSTEM IMPERATIVE — 147

THE INFORMATION SYSTEM SOLUTION IMPERATIVE	**148**
THE PRIMARY TASKS	148
Classification	149
Measurements	149
Presentation and Disclosures	149
Closing and Opening Balances	150
ACCOUNTING SOFTWARE SOLUTION	**150**

PREFACE

The **International Financial Reporting Standards (IFRS),** developed and administered by the **International Accounting Standard Board (IASB),** provide a globally acceptable uniform framework for the **preparation** and **presentation** of financial information of profit-oriented entities. About 145 countries have already adopted the standards, and many are in the process of doing so. Some of the big names in the list include major economies such as the European Union, Brazil, Canada, Australia, and Japan, among others. Although the United States has not officially adopted the IFRS as its primary accounting standard, in 2007, the SEC approved the use of IFRS for the filing of financial reports in the US by foreign quoted entities that use IFRS in their countries. In 2008, the SEC also presented a roadmap for adopting IFRS for all US publicly quoted companies. At the moment, companies within the US may choose to account for their finances under GAAP or IFRS.

The widespread adoption of IFRS has been driven by the need to create common global accounting and reporting standards to enhance transparency, comparability, and reliability of financial information across international borders. The pace of this drive was set by the global economic crisis of 2007 to 2009, which was largely attributed to fraudulent accounting practices.

The International Financial Reporting Standards (IFRS) was originally conceived and designed for quoted companies (companies listed on the Stock Exchange) where the requirements for accountability and transparency are of paramount importance to shareholders. The enormous cost of implementing full IFRS cannot be justified for Small and Medium Enterprises (SMEs), hence the need to issue a scaled-down version of IFRS that is suitable for Small and Medium Enterprises (SMEs).

The term SME has been defined differently by various jurisdictions, based on personnel size, annual turnover, or balance sheet total. However, none of these definitions is helpful when it comes to determining the eligibility for applying the IFRS for SMEs. According to IASB, IFRS for SMEs is designed for "**entities that have no public accountability.**" What this means is that any company not listed on the Stock Exchange, or not a Public Limited Company (PLC), is eligible to apply IFRS for SMEs. **Government Business Enterprises (GBEs)** are not eligible to apply IFRS for SMEs due to their obligation to render accounts to the government as well as the public. Therefore, all GBEs are to apply the full IFRS. However, it is also possible for national regulatory authorities to decide on the entities that should apply IFRS for SMEs and those that should not.

IFRS for SMEs is neither independent nor a separate set of standards although they have a separate framework. They are modifications and simplifications of the full Standards undertaken to make the Standards suitable and convenient for SMEs.

Irrespective of whether an entity is applying the full IFRS or the SME version, the task of implementing the standards and continued compliance with its accounting policies can be challenging, or even onerous. This book, which is a product of my more than ten years of field experience as an IFRS and IPSAS system specialist, is meant to address and ease the challenges of IFRS implementation and compliance.

This book is not a compendium of Standards under the IFRS; it is a practical guide to the accounting treatment, based on IFRS accounting policies. One thing that makes this book so different is its presentation format: it is not just about IFRS policies, but also the bookkeeping entries that accompany IFRS measurements—something one cannot find in any standard text on IFRS. All IFRS measurements are explained and backed up with relevant accounting entries in the double-entry format. I have also highlighted those areas where IFRS has been simplified for SMEs.

The book does not attempt to cover all the Standards and accounting policies under IFRS. I have selected those topics that are most relevant to small businesses. These include **Revenue** (IAS 18), **Construction Contracts** (IAS 11), **Inventory** (IAS 2), **Property, Plant and Equipment** (IAS 16), **Investment Property** (IAS 40), **Leases** (IAS 17) and **Presentation of Financial Statements** (IAS 1). I have also demonstrated the application of these Standards to such areas as accounting **Salary and Wages** and various forms of revenue and expense measurements and recognitions. **Value-Added Tax (VAT)** has been given special treatment because of the need to clarify all the issues involved in accounting for VAT.

In **Chapter 1**, I introduce the fundamental law and rules of accounting, along with the definitions of all the basic parameters that will guide us throughout the rest of the book. Try as much as possible to understand everything in this chapter because this chapter provides the foundation for the rest of the book.

Chapter 2 is on the **International Financial Reporting Standards (IFRS)**. IFRS has become the de facto accounting standard for the whole world, as nearly 300 countries have adopted the Standards or are in the process of doing so. This chapter provides a basic introduction to IFRS objectives and policies.

Chapter 3 deals with the traditional books of accounts, upon which the design and implementation of modern accounting systems rely so much on. It is one of the chapters meant to inform you about the old legacy that has shaped the practice of accounting.

Chapter 4 is concerned with the collating of all items to be accounted for and organizing them into a table called the **Chart of Accounts**. There are standard procedures for doing this, and this chapter will take you through everything you need to know about the Chart of Accounts. There is a sample Chart of Accounts for small businesses at the end of the chapter.

Chapter 5 introduces the recognition criteria for income and expense. You may wonder why. *Is there anybody who does not know what income is?* Well, the International Financial Reporting

Standards (IFRS) have specified a set of rules for the recognition of income and expense. The summary is: *It is not yet income until you have earned it, and it is not yet expense until you have incurred it*. This chapter will tell you everything about how it works under the IFRS standard IAS 18 (Revenue).

Chapter 6 is on revenue and expense recognition for **Construction Contracts**. Whereas IAS 18 takes care of revenue and expenses that are earned and incurred within one accounting period, Construction Contract (IAS 11) accounts for revenue and expenses that span accounting periods. The rules for measurement and recognition are different.

Chapter 7 is on **Inventory**. Accounting for goods is a completely different thing from accounting for services. All the relevant IFRS policies and associated accounting entries that apply to goods are discussed here.

Chapter 8 is on accounting for **Salary and Wages**. Both the employees and the employers are quite familiar with salary and wages, but what may not be so obvious are the accounting entries that must accompany them. This chapter takes you through the process of preparing and paying your salary, along with all the accounting entries that must be made.

Chapter 9 is on **Taxes**. It was Benjamin Franklin who stated in a letter he wrote to Jean-Baptiste Leroy, "In this world nothing is certain but death and taxes." No matter what happens, I just want you to understand the accounting entries required for taxes while we are still here.

Chapter 10 is about **Property, Plant, and Equipment**. We know them by the old and popular name, **Fixed Assets**. We need to account for, not only the initial cost we incur when we acquire them but also for the wears and tears that take place every day. This chapter takes care of all the mathematics and the accounting entries required.

Chapter 11 is on accounting for **Leases**. Lease accounting is like a coin: one piece with two different sides—but with each side obeying a different rule and policy. Here you will find explanations and accounting entries you may not be able to find elsewhere.

Chapter 12 is on the **Presentation of Financial Statements**. When it comes to accounting, you cannot convince anybody about what you are doing unless you can produce reports. Financial Statements make statements that breathe life into your data. This chapter explains the various reports and the minimum set of data that should appear in each of the reports.

Chapter 13 is on the **Cash Flows Statement**. Cash, they say is king. Perhaps, that is why the International Accounting Standards Board (IASB) has devoted one full Standard to it alone. And that may also be exactly why I am doing so here. This chapter explains the various types of cash flows and provides a practical guide on how to calculate cash flow.

Chapter 14 is on **Closing the Books**. It is the end of another accounting year! What do we do before we go home to celebrate? This chapter tells you everything you need to know and do to bring one accounting year to an end and begin another year.

Chapter 15 is on the **Information System Imperative** for accounting. I have decided to use this last chapter to tell you something about accounting software solutions, and this is my verdict: *You need accounting software. Your investment in accounting software will be more rewarding than whatever you are doing right now, or whatever anybody is telling you to do.*

This book is based on a solution algorithm by a software solution analyst, with several years of experience in the design, development, and implementation of accounting software for Small and Medium Enterprises (SMEs). The book has been made simpler than any accounting book in its category, with no prior knowledge of accounting assumed or required. It is meant to serve as a learning and a working manual for non-accountants and enthusiasts, especially owners of small businesses. Students and new accountants may also find the book useful as a companion text and a reference guide.

This book is based on the solution algorithm by a software solution analyst, with several years of experience in the design, development, and implementation of accounting software for Small and Medium Enterprises (SMEs). Industry professionals implementing IFRS, and students of accounting, will find this book quite helpful.

Etim O. Uso
etimuso@yahoo.com

+234(0)9132312209

ELEMENTS AND FUNDAMENTAL PRINCIPLES OF ACCOUNTING

Many people associate accounting with a profession or a career that requires years of a college education. You may be right, but this is only one side of the story. Accounting has a lot more to do with our daily lives than with a college education. Accounting is one language we all must learn, understand, and speak fluently because it is the language, as well as the tool, we use in all our financial transactions at personal and corporate levels.

Let us begin our journey into the world of accounting with the following introductory quests:

a) Understanding the full meaning of accounting and its methods.
b) Appreciating accounting and its relevance to our daily lives.
c) Understanding the basic elements, the law, and the rules of accounting so that we can apply them correctly.

WHAT IS ACCOUNTING?

Accounting is the process of **collecting, recording, processing,** and **presenting** financial data (primarily, in the form of financial statements) in a way that provides owners of businesses, investors (and sometimes, the general public) with reliable and accurate information about the financial status of the accounting **entity**. The first two tasks of collecting and recording financial data belong to what is called **Bookkeeping**.

What I want you to underline in this definition is the statement: *collation, preparation, and presentation of financial data to produce meaningful information.* This, essentially, constitutes what is called accounting.

If this definition sounds too formal—like something you are expected to regurgitate for your teacher in an exam—then let me put it in a different format. **Accounting is the science and art of measuring and managing wealth**. It is a science because it involves computations based on defined rules and principles; it is an art because certain aspects of it are subject to judgment and interpretation.

Accounting provides empirical and formal methods for the measurement and maintenance of the financial health of an organization (or an individual), based on standard measurements and parameters. **At the most basic level, accounting tells you where your money is coming from and where it is going**. Accounting is the barometer that gauges the financial status of your business and provides the information you need to manage your business successfully and profitably.

ACCOUNTING METHODS

Accounting is a process with standard methods of implementation. These methods specify the tasks to be carried out in an orderly sequence. We are going to look at the following four accounting methods: Classification, Measurements, Recognition, and Presentation.

CLASSIFICATION

Items to be accounted for must be classified according to standard categories and groups and listed orderly in a table called the **Chart of Accounts**. I will talk about these standard groups soon in this chapter, and the Chart of Accounts in Chapter 4.

MEASUREMENTS

Items to be recorded in the book of accounts must have values, and the values must be accurately measured based on standard rules. There are two types of measurements:

a) **Initial Measurement**—measurement (value) taken the first time the item is recognized and recorded in the book.
b) **Subsequent Measurement**—measurement (value) arrived at after the item has been in the book for a while. A typical example is the depreciation of fixed assets which gives rise to a Net Book Value (NBV) different from the purchase cost. We will encounter this in Chapter 10.

One obvious rule of accounting is you cannot account for something if you cannot measure it, or if you cannot determine its value.

RECOGNITION

There are defined criteria for recognizing every value obtained from accounting measurements. Items can only be recognized as assets, liability/equity, income, or expense after they have satisfied all set criteria for recognition. Timing is the most important criterion. For example, revenue from the sale of goods can only be recognized after the goods have been legally transferred to the buyer, and not when the buyer pays for the goods. We will be encountering more of these criteria throughout this book.

PRESENTATION

The presentation encompasses standard reports and notes you present to owners of the business, investors, regulators, and the public, whenever the need arises. Presentation is what gives substance and meaning to your classification and measurements.

There are standard reports, with defined structure and format, every accounting system is expected to produce. The most important ones (for profit-oriented entities) are as follows:

a) **Statement of Financial Position** (also called, Balance Sheet).
b) **Statement of Comprehensive Income** (also called, Income Statement).
c) **Statement of Cash Flows**.
d) **Statement of Changes in Equity**.

We will be dealing more with each of these reports in Chapter 13.

WHY ACCOUNTING?

Proper accounting is not only good for you and your business; it is also good for your partners, your customers, your employees, and the society you belong to. Accounting raises the level of confidence and trust people have in what you are doing. People who may want to invest in your business would like to know how your business is performing by looking at your books. Banks have been attributing their unwillingness to lend money to small businesses to poor accounting. Accounting will help you know almost all the variables that affect your business and finances, and how to monitor and control them.

Some of us are probably richer than we think. By the time you start keeping track of all your earnings and expenses, you will have a clearer picture of what you are worth (or ought to be). And, perhaps, such a picture may compel you to make conscious efforts and the decision to take full control of your finances through proper accounting.

ELEMENT OF FINANCIAL STATEMENTS

The financial statements of every accounting entity (whether manual- or computer-based) are structured and built around key elements (also referred to as **elements of financial statements**). These are the parameters that provide the framework for all accounting classification, measurement, and presentation. Let us look at those parameters.

ASSET

Assets are the resources—tangible or intangible—owned or controlled by an entity from which economic benefits are expected to flow into the entity, now or in the future. Those assets that can easily be converted to cash within the same accounting year (such as cash and bank deposits, customers' receivables, and inventories) are classified as **Current Assets**, while those that cannot be converted to cash within the same accounting year (such as property, plant, and equipment) are called **Fixed Assets** (or **Noncurrent Assets**).

LIABILITY

Liabilities are claims or debts against the assets that the entity is expected to settle, resulting in the outflow of resources from the entity. These include items, such as money you owe your suppliers or vendors (Trade Payables or Creditors), loans and borrowings you must pay back, taxes collected on behalf of the government, etc. Liabilities meant to be settled within one accounting year (such as creditors' payments) are classified as **Current Liabilities**, while those that may take more than one accounting year to settle (such as long-term debts or loans) are classified as **Long-term Liabilities**.

EQUITY

This represents the contributions of the owners of the business, as well as what is left for owners of the business when Liability is subtracted from Asset.

The **Balance sheet** (or **Statement of Financial Position**) is the financial report that provides information about the value of an entity's assets, liabilities, and equities. This report must satisfy the fundamental accounting equation:

Total Assets = Total Liabilities + Total Equity

We can also compute other parameters by simply changing the subject of this formula. Thus:

Total Equity = Total Assets + Total Liabilities

When you hear people say, "Account is not balanced," what they mean is that this equation has failed. And whenever this happens, it means the law of *double-entry* has been breached. We will soon look at the Double-Entry Principle.

INCOME

Any increase in assets or decrease in liability will generate income. Income is defined as the **increase in economic benefits** within one accounting period—excluding equity contributions from owners of the business. If this sounds too formal, then let me put it this way: *Income includes the value of all the goods you have sold, the services you have rendered, the interest you have earned, the royalties you have received, etc.—including those that have been paid for in cash and those not yet paid for.*

THE DIFFERENCE BETWEEN INCOME AND REVENUE

You may have, probably, come across the words *Income* and *Revenue* before and assumed both mean the same thing. Or you may have asked the question: *"What is the difference between Income and Revenue?"*

Income is defined as an "increase in economic benefits in the form of inflows or enhancements of assets or decreases in liabilities that result in increases in equity, other than contributions from equity holders" during a specified period. **Revenue**, on the other hand, is that part of income that is attributed to the ordinary activities of an entity (and excludes **Gains** such as profit on the disposals of noncurrent assets, foreign exchange translation, fair value adjustments, etc.). Thus,

Income= Revenue + Gains.

Now, let us forget about all that jargon and say something that is practically discernible: *If you are a commodity trader, all the inflows from the sale of your commodity are Revenue, but inflows from sources other than the sale of your commodity—such as interest from savings, dividends, gains from the sale of assets—are not part of your revenue. But when you add all these extras to your Revenue it becomes what is called Income.* Thus, we can say:

Income = Revenue + Inflows from other sources (such as interests, dividends, gains, etc.)

Therefore, Revenue is a subset of Income. However, note that what we consider Revenue is relative. Revenue is what you earn from selling the primary goods and services your business was set up to provide. That means if you are running a bank or a lending institution, *interest* is part of your revenue; if you are a Venture Capitalist or Equity Investor, *dividend* is part of your Revenue. But if you are in the oil and gas business, everything you get from hydrocarbon sales is your revenue, while whatever you get from the sale or lease of your assets is not. In this book, I will be using the two terms 'Revenue' and 'Income' interchangeably, but in your Chart of Accounts (see Chapter 4), make sure you separate **Revenue** from **Other Income** and disclose them separately in your Income Statement.

However, for public institutions that apply the International Public Sectors Accounting Standards (IPSAS), there is no clear distinction between Revenue and Income—everything is often classified as Revenue—except for profit-making public sector entities, classified as Government Business Entities (GBE). All GBEs are required to comply with the International Financial Reporting Standards (IFRS)—not IPSAS.

EXPENSE

Any decrease in assets or increase in liability will generate expense—which is defined as **decreases in economic benefits** within one accounting period, excluding equity disbursements to owners of the business.

Let me restate this without the jargon: **Expense** is the value of what you spend to keep your business going—whether already paid for in cash or not. It includes the outflows resulting from purchases of goods and services that are consumed in the course of the business (such as stationery, rents, electricity, etc.) within one accounting year and those that are deployed for the production and provision of goods and services (such as cars, machinery, buildings, etc.). Strictly, expenses on consumable items are classified as **Overhead Expenses**, while expenses on procurement of assets needed for production or capital appreciation (such as property, plant, and equipment) are called **Capital Expenses** or **Costs**.

Both the Income and Expenses are normally classified under one major group called **Profit or Loss Account** in the Chart of Accounts.

The **Income Statement** (or **Statement of Comprehensive Income**) report provides information on the performance of an entity, regarding whether the entity is making a profit or loss. Chapter 5 is devoted to the criteria for the recognition and measurement of income and expense.

UNDERSTANDING DEBIT AND CREDIT

The terms **debit** and **credit** are two terms you may have come across before. In ordinary usage, *debit* tends to connote a debt or something negative, while *credit* connotes something positive. Unfortunately, even the dictionary meanings of these words are not very helpful.

Now, let us look at the mathematical or accounting meaning of **debit** and **credit** in the context of **asset** and **liability, income,** and **expense**—the primary elements of accounting.

Debit implies an **increase in Assets** or a **decrease in Liability**. Thus, since sales increase your cash (asset) you will have to **debit your cash** account whenever you make a cash sale or **debit your**

customer (again, asset) for every credit sale. I will be using the notation **Dr.** to denote Debit in this book.

Credit implies an **increase in Liability** or **decrease in Assets**. Since credit purchase increases your liability, you will have to **credit the vendor's** or **supplier's account** whenever you buy anything on credit. Whenever you settle the debt by paying out cash, you will have to **credit your cash account** (which reduces your assets) and, correspondingly, **debit your vendor's account** to reduce your liability. I will be using the notation **Cr.** to denote Credit in this book.

The table below summarizes the relationships between **debit** and **credit** with respect to the primary elements of the accounting system:

Parameter	Debit	Credit
Asset	Increase	Decrease
Liability/Equity	Decrease	Increase
Income	Decrease	Increase
Expense	Increase	Decrease

With this very important background information and the simple arithmetic, let us now go ahead and look at the most important law or principle of modern accounting.

THE FUNDAMENTAL LAW AND PRINCIPLES OF ACCOUNTING

No system can function effectively without some fundamental principle or law to regulate its existence. Most laws give rise to corollaries, thereby making it possible to construct other rules, because of the law. I have said that accounting can also be regarded as a science because it involves computation based on well-defined rules and principles. In this section, I will take you through the law of accounting, as well as those basic principles that qualify accounting as a science.

The rules and methods of accounting may be subject to review, but the fundamental law of accounting will always remain the same, irrespective of whether the system is based on GAAP (Generally Accepted Accounting Principles) or IFRS (International Financial Reporting Standards). The **double-entry** accounting principle, developed in 1340, remains the fundamental law of modern accounting.

THE LAW OF DOUBLE-ENTRY

Modern accounting is based on a law, often referred to as the ***double-entry principle***. The double-entry principle can be viewed in two parts. The principal part deals with the individual transaction or accounting entries, while the second part (the corollary) deals with the entire book (all the Ledgers combined).

Under the double-entry principle, every accounting transaction will result in at least two entries: the **debit**(s) part and the **credit**(s) part (I have already explained what the terms *debit* and *credit* mean).

The double-entry principle states that **for any given accounting transaction the sum of all debit entries must be equal to the sum of all credit entries, and vice versa:**

    1)   Total Debit(s) = Total Credit(s)

In other words, every ***debit*** entry (or entries) must have a corresponding ***credit*** entry (or entries), and vice versa.

If we regard the first equation as the basic law of accounting, then the corollary to this law is the one that states that the sum of all **Assets** must be equal to the sum of all **Liabilities** plus **Equity**:

    2)   Total Assets = Total Liabilities + Total Equity

It is a corollary because if the first equation is satisfied for all the transactions, then the second one will follow, invariably.

In practice, these two laws form the basis of the following financial reports: the **Trial Balance** and the **Balance Sheet (Statement of Financial Position)**. While the Trial Balance is used to check the accuracy of data entry (whether all the debit and credit entries sum up to zero), the Balance Sheet gives a clearer picture of the distribution of the entity's assets, liabilities, and equities.

When all the accounting entries comply with these two laws, the balance resulting from subtracting all the credit entries from all the debit entries will be zero; the balance resulting from subtracting the total of all the liabilities from the total of all the assets will be the *equity*. If any of these fails, then there is a problem, and the accountant must find the cause of the problem and fix it. You must have heard of the statement "account is not balanced!" It is bad news that means the account has not satisfied the law of double-entry.

HOW DOUBLE-ENTRY RESONATES WITH THE NATURAL LAWS...

The double-entry accounting principle is not just an academic theory; it is a scientific formulation that conforms to the natural law of nature. Apart from providing an empirical and universal way of measuring wealth, it has also provided us ethical basis and method for enforcing accountability at public, corporate, and private levels.

The law compels us to account for both the *sources* and *destinations* (or uses) of money and to make sure what comes in and what goes out balance off. That, to me, is the basic principle of accountability. This may not prevent fraud completely, but it will help trace and locate the *sink*. It will also help in the design and implementation of control measures.

We can also see similarities between this accounting law and **Newton's Third Law of Motion**, namely, "*action and Reaction are equal and opposite*." The **First Law of Thermodynamics** states that "*matter can neither be created nor destroyed, but can only be transformed...*" So if we consider the amount of money in circulation as fixed, you can see how the double-entry principle conforms to the natural order of things. You can also see why there will be inflation if governments just go ahead and print money whenever they need money. This is why I choose to refer to double-entry as a "law" and not just a principle. It is a fundamental law upon which modern accounting and economy derive their legitimacy and control mechanism.

PRACTICAL EXAMPLES WITH DOUBLE-ENTRY POSTINGS

Let me use the following practical examples to illustrate the double-entry accounting format:
If you go to the bank and withdraw $1000, you will have to make an entry in your book to indicate the withdrawal of $1000 from your account. The second part requires the recognition of receipt of $1000 cash. The *source* here is the **Bank** account, and the *destination* is the **Cash** account. In accounting terms, the transaction above can be translated as follows: **debit** *Cash* (to increase your asset) and **Credit** *Bank* (to reduce your asset) each with the $1000:

      Dr.   Cash
      Cr.   Bank

The story of the $1000 does not end here. You will have to continue accounting for subsequent transactions involving the $1000 cash.
Assuming, for example, you buy a pair of shoes for $350. You will have to indicate that $350 has left your hand to some *destination* (in this case, the *purchase of shoes*). In accounting terms, you will *debit* Expenses (shoes) and *credit* Cash:

> Dr. Expense (Shoes)
> Cr. Cash

You will repeat similar entries each time you spend the $1000. At any point the total amount you spend plus the cash you have left should be equal to the initial amount you received—in this case, $1000.

Now, let us consider another example involving Ms. Ann, who is starting a new business with the sum of $50,000. Ms. Ann opened a bank account and deposited the $50,000 (let us forget about where the money is coming from—all we know is that Ms. Ann is starting her business with $50,000 capital).

From this amount, Ms. Ann made the following purchases and drawings:

1) Office Furniture   7,000
2) Computers   17,500
3) Office Stationery   1,000
4) Petty Cash   1,000
5) Ms. Ann also received goods worth $10,000 which she intends to sell (but has not yet paid for) from Elite Pharmaceuticals Inc.

Assuming that we are not interested in where the initial capital of $50,000 came from, our first entry will be to **Debit Bank** and **Credit Capital** with this amount used in starting the business:

> Dr. Bank
> Cr. Capital

For the subsequent transactions, we will make the following entries:

Office Furniture

    Dr.   : Fixed Assets (Furniture)
    Cr.   : Bank

Computers
    Dr.   : Fixed Assets (Office Equipment)
    Cr.   : Bank

Office Stationery
    Dr.   : Stationery (Profit and Loss Expense account)
    Cr.   : Bank

Petty Cash
    Dr.   : Petty Cash
    Cr.   : Bank

Goods
    Dr.   Inventory
    Cr.   Elite Pharmaceuticals Inc.

Note that in each case, we take from the initial money that was used in starting the business.

All these entries are nothing more than pieces of data. They do not provide meaningful information as to what is happening to the business in terms of its assets, liabilities, income, expenses, etc. This is where Presentation (Reports, Notes) comes in as one of the key components of accounting.

    Let us, first look at the Journal entries and then see how we can extract reports that will give us a good picture of what is happening:

TRANSACTION	DEBIT	CREDIT
Capital		
Bank	50,000	
Initial/Share Capital		50,000
Purchase of Fixed Assets		
Furniture	7,000	
Office Equipment	17,500	
Bank		24,500
Purchase of Stationery (Profit or Loss)		
Stationery	1,000	

Bank		1,000
Petty Cash (Cashbook)		
Petty Cash	1,000	
Bank		1,000
Purchase of Goods on Credit		
Inventory	10,000	
Trade Payable (Elite Pharmaceuticals Inc.)		10,000
TOTAL	**86,500**	**86,500**

In the end, you can see that the total of all the **debits** is equal to the total of all the **credits** in compliance with the law of Double-entry. And we can happily say that the account is "balanced!"

Now let us extract the **Statement of Financial Position (Balance Sheet)** by computing the balance for each of the major accounts. Note that this going to be a manual report; in a computerized accounting system, this report can be filtered to show either the summary or the detailed elements of the transactions.

ACCOUNT	DEBIT BALANCE	CREDIT BALANCE
CAPITAL		
Initial/Share Capital		50,000
FIXED ASSETS		
Furniture	7,000	
Office Equipment	17,500	
INVENTORY		
Finished Goods	10,000	
CASH & CASH EQUIVALENTS		
Petty Cash	1,000	
Bank	23,500	
TRADE PAYABLES		
Elite Pharmaceuticals Inc.		10,000

PROFIT OR LOSS BROUGHT FORWARD Expense	1,000	
TOTAL	60,000	60,000

Again, you can say "The account is balanced!"

I have used the term **Profit or Loss Brought Forward** here without defining it. Income and Expense are not usually presented on the face of the Statement of Financial Position (Balance Sheet); it is the Profit or Loss (Income - Expense) that is usually reported as Profit or Loss Brought Forward, or simply as **Retained Earnings**. That is why you may have heard your CPA say, "Income and Expenses are not Balance Sheet items." We will look at this topic in detail in Chapter 13.

KEY ASSUMPTIONS IN ACCOUNTING

Two basic assumptions underlie the preparation and presentation of financial statements by profit-oriented entities. They are **Accrual Basis** and **Going Concern**.

ACCRUAL BASIS

Accrual basis accounting stipulates that transactions (particularly revenue and expense) are recognized and recorded in the accounting period in which they occur (and not when cash is paid or received). This contrasts with **cash-basis** accounting which recognizes revenue only when cash is received and expense when cash is paid.

GOING CONCERN

It is assumed that the entity is currently in operation (is not under liquidation or has any intention of going into liquidation) and will continue to remain so for the foreseeable future.

Under the International Financial Reporting Standards (IFRS), financial statements prepared and presented by an entity cannot be said to be valid or in conformity with the rules of accounting, if these two assumptions are not met.

THE INTERNATIONAL FINANCIAL REPORTING STANDARDS (IFRS)

A common set accounting standards for the whole world has finally become a reality. No more national GAAP (Generally Accepted Accounting Principles) and all the loopholes. Almost 300 countries (including the EU countries) have already adopted the International Financial Reporting Standards (IFRS) or are in the process of doing so. Although the United States has not officially adopted the IFRS as its primary accounting standard, in 2007, the SEC approved the use of IFRS for the filing of financial reports in the US by foreign quoted entities that use IFRS in their countries. In 2008, the SEC also presented a roadmap for adopting IFRS for all US publicly quoted companies. At the moment, companies within the US may choose to account for their finances under GAAP or IFRS.

The world has witnessed chaos, and even scandals, resulting from accounting improprieties, some of which were considered normal in some jurisdictions. However, the last financial crisis, which virtually affected the whole world, gave rise to the urgent need to curtail some of these improprieties. Now to remove all the grey areas, the world is gradually moving towards common, universally acceptable rules and methods for accounting and financial reporting. That is what the **International Financial Reporting Standards (IFRS)** are meant to achieve.

The **International Financial Reporting Standards (IFRS)** provide a globally acceptable uniform framework for the **preparation** and

presentation of financial information of profit-oriented entities. **IFRS** is developed and administered by the **International Accounting Standard Board (IASB)** based in London. IASB also administers **International Accounting Standards (IAS)**, which it inherited from its predecessor, the Board of the **International Accounting Standards Committee**.

The name, International Financial Reporting Standards (IFRS), sounds like a misnomer because the standards encompass much more than financial reporting. IFRS also prescribes rules and criteria for recognition, classification, and measurements. The former name, International Accounting Standards (IAS), was more apt.

In some areas, the differences between IFRS and GAAP are not too significant, but in other areas, the differences are significant enough to warrant a new set of measurements and recognition policies. But when it comes to the area of disclosure (presentation of financial statements and notes) the difference between IFRS and GAAP is huge. The disclosure requirements under IFRS are more extensive and rigorous.

THE STANDARDS

The term **International Financial Reporting Standards (IFRS)** includes the following:

- **New Standards** (comprising IFRS 1 to 16—new Standards are being added every year).

- **Improvements to IAS** (IAS 1, 2, 7, 8, 10, 11, 12, 18, 20, 21, 23, 24, 27, 28, 29, 31, 32, 33, 34, 36, 37, 38, 39, 40 and 41) from the ISAB's Improvement Project of 2003. Some of the listed IASs have already been slated for future replacement with new IFRSs. For example, IFRS 15 will replace IAS 18 in 2018; IFRS 16 will replace IAS 27 in 2019.

- **International Financial Report Interpretations Committee (IFRIC) Interpretations** (comprising of the following chapters IFRIC 1-21).

- **Standing Interpretations Committee (SIC) Interpretations** (comprising of the following chapters: SIC 1-3, 5-33). Note that IFRIC replaced SIC in 2002.

The numbering of these Standards and Interpretations keeps changing, as new Standards are being added and old ones improved and renamed. This was the situation in 2015 when this book was first written. Do not be surprised if some of these numbers are changed by the time you read this book.

IASB'S OBJECTIVE

The IASB's objective includes the development of "high-quality global accounting standards" that will engender transparent reporting, and make it possible to compare financial information globally, in the interest of the general public.

According to IASB's Framework, the objective of financial statements is to provide information that might be useful to users of financial information in making decisions about the entity. Such information must include the financial position, performance, and changes in the financial position of an entity. Users of such information include current and future investors, employees, creditors, debtors, governments, and the general public.

Part of IASB's policies towards achieving its objective is the prescription of uniform accounting policies for *like transactions and events* both within an entity (and among entities).

IASB intends not to permit choices in accounting treatment. This, perhaps, is due to the general observation that the accounting choices of many entities are influenced more by tax considerations than the faithful presentation of facts on the ground. However, IASB has reconsidered and will continue to reconsider those transactions and events for which choices in accounting treatment should be permitted with the intention of reducing such choices.

FIRST-TIME ADOPTION OF THE IFRS

Before the full transition to IFRS, each entity is required to apply all relevant IFRS Standards retrospectively as of the Closing Balance Sheet date for its first IFRS financial statements before the transition date. This implies that IFRS standards should be applied as if the company had always been reporting under IFRS on that date.

The following are some of the key tasks that need to be performed as part of the first-time adoption project:

1) Quantifying all the adjustments to be carried out based on IFRS measurement and recognition criteria.
2) Create templates for IFRS financial statements.
3) Identify and fill all data gaps.
4) Establish an IFRS reporting process.
5) Prepare and produce initial IFRS financial statements.

IFRS 1 (First-Time Adoption of International Reporting Standards) documents all the requirements for all first-time adopters of the IFRS.

SPECIFIC IFRS REQUIREMENTS FOR FIRST-TIME ADOPTER

IFRS 1 prescribes the following adjustments at the time of transiting from the previous GAAP to IFRS:

1) **Recognize** all assets, liability/equity, revenue, and expenses whose recognitions are required under IFRS.
2) **Derecognize** items of asset, liability/equity, revenue, and expense if IFRS does not permit such recognition.
3) **Reclassify** items that are recognized under previous GAAP as one type of asset, liability, or component of equity, but are a different type under IFRS.
4) **Measure** all recognized assets and liabilities according to principles enshrined in the Standards and the Framework.

In addition, the IFRS requires disclosures that explain how the transition from previous GAAP to IFRS affected the entity's reported financial position, financial performance, and cash flows.

IFRS COMPLIANCE REQUIREMENTS

For an entity transiting from other accounting standards to the IFRS to be considered to have complied with the IFRS, the entity must meet the following key requirements:

1) Select appropriate IFRS Policies.
2) Design and document internal practices, guidelines, and procedures to reflect the new accounting policies to ensure proper and consistent application of the policies.
3) Recognize all assets and liabilities in compliance with IFRS requirements.
4) Classify or reclassify all assets and liabilities according to IFRS requirements.
5) Apply the IFRS rule or policy in measuring all recognized assets and liabilities.
6) Make all accounting adjustments and reconciliations needed to convert from GAAP to IFRS.
7) Create IFRS financial statements and reporting process to support the statements.

Generally, the fundamental requirements for IFRS compliance, as set out by each Standard, can be summarized based on standard accounting methods as follows:

Recognition and Classification

Asset, liability/equity, revenue, and expenditure must be recognized based strictly on IFRS requirements and criteria for recognition, and the recognized item must be classified based on rules stipulated by the relevant Standards. For example, revenue for the Construction of Real Estate (IFRIC 15) can be recognized as:

   a) Construction Contract (IAS 11).
   b) Sale of Goods (IAS 18).
   c) Provision of Service (IAS 18).

Each of these recognitions and classifications depends on the construction agreement.

Initial and Subsequent Measurements

After recognition, it is necessary to measure and determine the value of the asset, liability, or equity based on one of the accepted measurement bases (cost, fair value, etc.). Subsequently, the value of the item must be determined based on selected measurement bases and accounting policies or rules for each class of asset, liability, and equity.

Presentation & Disclosure

Apart from the general requirements of **IAS 1 (Presentation of Financial Statements)** which prescribes the format and the minimum contents of financial statements along with all the general disclosures, each Standard prescribes specific items to be disclosed and presented by the preparers of financial statements. Some of these items are required either on the face of the financial statements or as notes to be attached to the financial statements.

IFRS FOR SMEs

The International Financial Reporting Standards (IFRS) was originally conceived and designed for quoted companies (companies listed in the Stock Exchange) where the requirements for accountability and transparency are of paramount importance to shareholders. The enormous cost of implementing full IFRS cannot be justified for small and medium enterprises (SMEs), hence the need for a scaled-down version of IFRS that is suitable for SMEs.

The reporting requirements for quoted companies and companies with significant public interests are designed to cater to the information needs of shareholders and the investing public. The accounting policies and reporting requirements of Small and Medium Enterprises (SMEs) are not expected to be as rigorous as those of quoted entities due to differences in their reporting goals and business models. It is for these and a few other reasons the International Accounting Standards Board (IASB) issued an alternative framework for the formulation of International Financial Accounting Standards for SMEs.

IFRS for SMEs is neither independent nor a separate set of standards although they have a separate framework. They are modifications and simplifications of the full Standards undertaken to make the Standards suitable and convenient for SMEs.

WHAT IS SME?

The term, SME (Small and Medium Enterprises), has been defined differently by various jurisdictions based on personnel size, annual turnover, or balance sheet total. However, none of these definitions is helpful when it comes to determining the eligibility for applying IFRS for SMEs.

According to IASB, IFRS for SMEs is designed for "**entities that have no public accountability.**" What this means is that any company not listed on the Stock Exchange, or not a Public Limited

Company (PLC), is eligible to apply IFRS for SMEs. **Government Business Enterprises (GBEs)** are not eligible to apply IFRS for SMEs due to their obligation to render accounts to the government as well as the general public. Therefore, all GBEs are to apply the full IFRS. However, it is also possible for national regulatory authorities to decide on the entities that should apply IFRS for SMEs and those that should not.

WHY IFRS FOR SMES?

As I stated earlier, IFRS was designed primarily for quoted companies. The accounting requirements and reporting needs of SMEs are different from those of quoted companies. IFRS for SMEs was issued to address the peculiar needs of small businesses.

One other important factor that necessitated the issuance of a separate set of standards for SMEs is the cost-benefit consideration for financial reporting. IASB has made it clear that *the benefits derived from financial information should not exceed the cost of providing it*. For SMEs, It is impossible to justify the enormous cost involved in applying the full IFRS with all the rigorous accounting treatments and disclosure requirements.

IFRS for SMEs is a modified version of the full IFRS. The modification has been achieved through the following process of omission and simplification:

1) Some Standards or topics that are not relevant to the accounting needs of SMEs are omitted.
2) Some accounting policies are either not allowed or alternative options are provided.
3) Some recognition and measurement criteria are simplified.
4) There are fewer disclosure requirements.

Items omitted include:

a) Earnings per Share (IAS 33).

b) Interim Financial Reporting (IAS 34).
c) Segment Reporting (IFRS 8).
d) Insurance Contracts (IFRS 4).
e) Assets Held for Sale (IFRS 5).

Some of the areas of simplification include:

a) Accounting treatments and policies.
b) Recognition and measurement rules.
c) Disclosure requirements.

Specific Standards that are affected by these simplifications in recognition and measurement are as follows:

1) Financial Instruments (IAS 39).
2) Property, Plant, and Equipment (IAS 16).
3) Investment Property (IAS 40).
4) Intangible Assets (IAS 38).
5) Defined Benefits (IAS 19).
6) Biological Assets (IAS 41).

It is not possible to provide full details of all the recognition and measurement issues involved in IFRS for SMEs in this book. SMEs are free to choose between applying the full IFRS or IFRS for SMEs. However, whichever option the entity elects to apply, it must apply all of it in full without mixing the requirements of the two Standards. All the accounting treatments in this book comply with full IFRS policies.

THE BOOKS OF ACCOUNTS

Accounting and bookkeeping are age-old practices that have been developed over the years and handed down to us. Unlike many other fields, such as information technology or the auto industry, where change is a constant keyword, accounting has remained fairly unchanged for centuries. The books of accounts form part of the traditional rules we must learn, understand, and conform to. But how practically relevant are these books to us today?

In the early days when everything was done manually, accounting was a tedious process, even for small businesses with very limited transactions. Several books must be kept; entries must be transferred from one book to another until you arrive at what is called the General Ledger. Organizational workflows and structures were designed and set up to mimic the various books of accounts (or is it the other way around?). Even modern accounting software is modeled along the lines of these traditional books of accounts. In this chapter, we shall look at the standard books of accounts.

THE BOOKS OF ACCOUNTS

The standard books of accounts (also called, the **Ledgers**) are as follows:

1) The Journal
2) The Cashbook

3) Accounts Receivable (Debtors or Sales Ledger)
4) Accounts Payable (Creditors or Purchases Ledger)
5) Inventory Control
6) Fixed Assets

Depending on its size, organizational structure, and control mechanisms, an entity may choose to maintain other books besides the major ones listed here. Each book keeps a record of daily transactions in the following format:

a) Transaction Date
b) Transaction ID
c) Voucher Type
d) Voucher Number
e) Narration
f) Debit
g) Credit

Some systems may provide additional data fields, and some may choose to collapse the *Debit* and *Credit* columns into one and label it *Amount*.

Let us look at each of these books in detail to understand the type of information that should go into each of them.

THE JOURNAL

Under the manual bookkeeping system, the **Journal** is regarded as the book of primary or original entry—where the various transactions are first recorded in the order in which they occur before they are transferred to their respective Ledgers. Entries in the Journal may comprise the following data fields: *Date, Narration, Account,* and *Amount*. At the end of the day entries from the Journal are summarized and posted to their respective books or Ledgers. The role of the Journal in a computerized accounting system is somewhat different.

CASHBOOK

The Cashbook is used to record all the transactions involving cash/cheque **receipts** and **payments**. All the amounts received are entered in the *debits* column, while payments go to the *credits* side.

ACCOUNTS RECEIVABLE

Accounts Receivable, also known as **Sales** or **Debtors Ledger**, is used for recording all credit sales and cash receipts from customers. This is a two-phase transaction which involves:

a) Recording the sales first as a *debit* entry against the customer, and
b) Recording cash receipts from customers for outstanding debt as *credit* entries.

ACCOUNTS PAYABLE

Accounts Payable, also known as **Purchase** or **Creditors Ledger**, is used to record all credit purchases and payments. Purchases are entered as *credit* entries in the vendor's or supplier's account, while payments are recorded as *debits*.

INVENTORY

The Inventory control ledger keeps a record of all the purchases of goods, as well as goods sold or issued. You will find detailed accounting treatments for Inventory in Chapter 7.

FIXED ASSETS

The fixed assets ledger keeps a record of all purchases and disposals of tangible assets, such as cars and machinery.

Depreciation (which represents wear and tear) on these items is computed on a monthly (or yearly) basis and posted as the expense for the period. You will find detailed accounting treatments for fixed assets in Chapter 10.

The entries from each Ledger are routinely summarized and aggregated under each account and posted into another book called the **General Ledger**. Thus, the General Ledger can be regarded as the hub of all the other ledgers or the master ledger. Each ledger is designed to capture as many details as possible, while the general ledger contains just the balance for each account. In a manual accounting system, most of all the standard reports such as the **Balance Sheet** and **Income Statement** are extracted from General Ledger.

COMPUTER-BASED ACCOUNTING SYSTEM

Segregating accounting tasks into these books remains the most effective form of internal control where several people are involved in carrying out different tasks. In a manual accounting situation, we are not just dealing with tasks, we are also dealing with physical books or ledgers where somebody must write down something.

But in a computerized system, where accounting software is used, the books become virtual forms or folders—they may not really exist as separate units. However, you may have distinct modules such as *Accounts Payable,* but your *debit* and *credit* entries end up in one common data table as line items. This data is filtered out as reports when you request for, say, Debtors' Ledger. What you call the General Ledger is nothing but a report showing all the balances grouped by accounts. Journals are now playing a less significant role, with *vouchers*, *invoices,* and *receipts* functioning as the source documents that provide the original data inputted directly into the computer.

While these books may continue to remain the basis for structuring the accounts department and designing internal controls, we should start seeing them as relics of the past from the days of manual accounting. We should be less rigid in enforcing the rules, especially with small businesses where one person may have to perform several functions. Software models based on functional classes or activities that represent the key elements of financial statements may be easier to understand than ledger-based systems.

THE CHART OF ACCOUNTS

Accounting involves keeping track of items with known monetary values. You cannot begin accounting without, first, compiling a list of all those items or activities you want to account for. Now is the time to collate and organize those items into a standard list, called the chart of accounts. You will not be able to track or account for any item not in this chart.

The Chart of Accounts is a table showing a line-by-line listing of all the items (accounts) that the entity wants to track in its books. Items in the Chart of Accounts are grouped based on the primary elements of financial statements—assets, liabilities, equity, income, expense, and their subgroups.

Each item (account) in the chart is assigned a unique code, followed by a descriptive name, in addition to base properties associated with each category of account. Additional properties such as the account's currency (in a multi-currency system) may also be required.

Items in the Chart of Accounts will differ from organization to organization, from industry to industry. There may also be differences in the size and complexity of the chart of accounts, depending on the activities of the organization. The basic rule is to make sure all the items you want to track are listed under the appropriate class in the Chart of Accounts. If, for example, you want to track the maintenance cost on each vehicle, then you will have to create an account for each vehicle under the general class "VEHICLE MAINTENANCE" which will belong to the primary class "EXPENSE" under the PROFIT OR LOSS group.

Any item you want to see in your financial statements and other financial reports as a line item should be included in the chart of accounts with a unique code. However, keep unnecessary details out of the chart of accounts. Details involving sales, purchases, inventory, customers, etc. should be confined to sub-ledgers or journals. Use your discretion while setting up your chart of accounts but ensure that you adhere strictly to the rules for classifying assets, liabilities, equities, income, and expenses. The basic format for the chart of accounts is as shown below:

Major/Sub Classes	Account Code	Description
xxx	xxx-yyy	zzz

Each account should be associated with one of the following classes and sub-classes:

Major Class	Sub Class
ASSET	**Current Assets** This includes Inventory, Cash, Trade Receivables/Debtors, Prepaid Expenses, etc.
	Non-current Assets Also called Fixed Assets, it includes items such as Plants and Machinery, Motor Vehicles, Lands and Buildings, Investments, Goodwill, etc.
LIABILITY	**Current Liabilities** Includes such items as Trade Payable/Creditors, short-term Loans Deferred Earnings, etc.
	Long-Term Liabilities (Such as Long-term Loans and other long-term obligations)

EQUITY	Share Capital
	Retained Earnings
	Reserves
INCOME	Sales Revenue
	Other Income
EXPENSE	Direct Cost
	Overhead Expense

ACCOUNTS CODING CONVENTION

Most charts of accounts use code to represent each account. Although some systems may not use codes to represent accounts, I strongly recommend the use of code to avoid possible duplication and conflicting account names.

What is the best approach to adopt in assigning codes to accounts? There are no fixed rules when it comes to accounts coding method, but I have always adopted the following coding convention in most of the systems I have designed and implemented:

1) Maintain consistency in coding based on system-defined sequence, and user-defined parameters.
2) Assign the codes in such a way that they can be generated automatically. This is very important in a large system where there are so many accounts to create, and more than one person is involved in creating accounts.

Here is the format for my preferred coding convention:

a) The major and subaccount classes are identified by a fixed number of numeric digits (say, 3 digits)
b) Another set of numeric digits is used to represent each account under the class (say, 5 digits)

c) A hyphen or a dot separates the account class from the account.

This coding convention will result in the following format: **xxx-xxxxx**.

Based on the above coding convention, if you assign the number 001 to CASH and the digit 000003 to PETTY CASH, then the full account code for **Petty Cash** will appear as 001-00003. The sample chart of accounts below uses this convention.

SAMPLE CHART OF ACCOUNTS

The table below is designed to demonstrate the structure of the chart of accounts. The line items may be different for each entity—depending on the operation, types of products, and services. Some entities may require additional subclasses and their list of accounts could be several pages long.

This is a partial list that should be treated as a sample designed to guide you in setting up your own chart of accounts. But note that some of the accounts listed here are standard accounts you must include in your chart of accounts. I have decided to use a bold typeface for those standard accounts.

Base Class	Sub-Class	Account Code	Account Description
Noncurrent Assets	Property, Plant and Equipment (PPE) 001	001-00001	Land
		001-00002	Building
		001-00003	Computer & Office Equipment
		001-00004	Furniture and Fittings
		001-00005	Plant and Equipment
		001-00006	Accumulated Depreciation – PPE

	Investment Property 002	002-00001 002-00002 002-00003	Land Building Accumulated Depreciation – Investment Property
	Intangible Assets 003	003-00001 003-00002 003-00003	Intellectual Property Trademarks and Patents Amortization of Intangible Assets
	Financial Assets 004		
	Biological Assets 005	005-00001 005-00002 005-00003	Living Animals and Plants Un-harvested Agricultural Produce Accumulated Depreciation – Biological Assets
Current Assets	Inventories 010	010-00001 010-00002 010-00003	Inventory - Raw Materials Inventory - Goods Inventory - Others
	Trade Receivables 011		(List all your customers here)
	Other Receivables 012	012-00001 012-00002 012-00003	VAT (Input) Receivable VAT Taken at Source Withholding Tax Receivable

	Cash and Cash Equivalents 013	013-00001 013-00002 013-00003	Petty Cash Till Cash Treasury Cash (Set up all your bank accounts here)
	Short-Term Investments 014	014-00001	Treasury Bills (Investments that are due to mature within one accounting year such as Placements)
	Employees Loans and Advances 015		(List your employees here)
	Prepayments 016	016-00001 016-00002 016-00003	Prepaid Rents Prepaid Insurance Prepaid Maintenance and Supports
	Noncurrent Assets Held For Sale 017		
Equity	Capital 025	025-00001 025-00002 025-00003	Share Capital Reserves Retained Earnings
	Other Components of Equity 026	026-00001 026-00002 026-00002	Exchange Rates Translation Differences Gains on Property Revaluation

				Available for Sale Financial Assets
Noncurrent Liabilities				
	Long-term Loans and Borrowings 030			(Loans and Borrowings to be repaid over a period of more than one year)
	Deferred Tax 031			
	Long-term Provisions 032			
	Other Noncurrent Liabilities 033			
Current Liabilities	**Trade Payables** 040			(List all your suppliers/vendors here)
	Other Payables 041	041-00001 041-00002 041-00003 041-00004		VAT (Output) Payable Withholding Tax Payable (Federal) Withholding Tax Payable (State) Income Tax Payable
	Payroll Liabilities 042	042-00001 042-00002 042-00003 042-00004		PAYE Tax Pension Staff Cooperative Payroll Clearing account
	Short-term Borrowings 043			(List all the loans and borrowings to be

			repaid within one year)
	Unearned Income 044	044-00001 044-00002 044-00003	Unearned Customer Loyalty Unearned Rents Unearned Maintenance and Support Revenue
	Short-term Provisions 045		
Income			
	Sales Revenue 100	100-00001 100-00002 100-00003	Sale of Goods Provision of Service Sales - Customer Loyalty
	Other Income 101	101-00001 101-00002 101-00003	Interests Earned Dividends Received Sundry Income
Expense	**Direct Cost (Cost of Sales)** 104	104-00001 104-00002 104-00003 104-00004	Cost of Goods Impairment Loss Sales Discount Other Direct Costs
	Distribution Costs 105		
	Finance Costs 106		(Interest on loans and borrowings)
	Personnel Costs 107	107-00001 107-00002 107-00003 107-00004 107-00005 107-00006	Basic Salary Housing Allowance Transport Allowance Utility Allowance Entertainment Allowance

		107-00007	Other Allowances
		107-00008	Overtime
		107-00009	Bonus
			Other Personnel Costs
	General and Admin Expenses 108	108-00001	Transportation Expense
		108-00002	VAT Expense
		108-00003	Employer's Pension Expense
		108-00004	
		108-00005	Company Income Tax
		108-00006	Rents
		108-00007	Bank COT
		108-00008	Other Bank Charges Etc...
	Other Expenses 110		(make sure you include all your items of expenditure in the chart under the appropriate group)

Note that the coding convention is user-defined. You can adopt whatever coding convention you consider convenient, but just ensure the codes are consistent and understandable. I have intentionally left some gaps in the chart so that you can fill in your unique items.

RECOGNITION AND MEASUREMENT OF REVENUE (AND EXPENSE)

In recent years the world has witnessed several high-profile financial scandals that have led to the collapse of great corporations, with devastating global consequences. Some of these collapses were very sudden and unexpected as most of these entities were posting healthy profits regularly. One of the factors in some of these scandals has been traced to accounting methods and policies, which permit the manipulation of financial figures through inappropriate and aggressive revenue recognition.

Revenue remains the most important item in the chart of accounts of all profit-oriented entities—irrespective of size, industry, or geographic location. A company is identified by its revenue streams more than anything else. This chapter will examine IFRS accounting policies (the measurements, recognition, and classification issues) for revenue. But before we do that, let us understand the difference between Revenue and Income.

In Chapter 1, I explained the difference between Revenue and Income, but in this chapter, I may be using the two terms—revenue and income—interchangeably. But in your chart of accounts, make sure you separate **revenue** from **other income**, and disclose it separately in your Income Statement.

RECOGNITION OF REVENUE

IAS 18 (Revenue) is the Standard that prescribes the criteria for the classification, measurement, recognition, and presentation of revenue (as well as expense). However, effective **IFRS 15** will replace IAS 18. The key issue with income or revenue recognition is timing—at what point in a transaction should an entity recognize revenue?

Specifically, **IAS 18** deals with the following types of revenue: **sales of goods**; **provision of services**; **royalties, and dividends**. It excludes income from other sources covered by different standards, such as Leases (IAS 27); dividends from equity method of investments (IAS 28); Insurance Contracts (IFRS 4); Changes in Fair Values of Financial Instruments (IAS 39), and current assets; Initial Recognition and Change in Fair Values of Biological Assets (IAS 41) and Initial Recognition of Agricultural Produce (IAS 41).

RECOGNITION OF REVENUE—SALE OF GOODS

Revenue from the **sales of goods** can only be recognized when the following conditions are met:

(a) The entity has transferred to the buyer the significant risks and rewards of ownership of goods.
(b) The entity retains neither continuing managerial involvement to the degree usually associated with ownership nor effective control over the goods sold.
(c) The amount of revenue can be measured reliably.
(d) It is probable that the economic benefits associated with the transaction will flow to the entity.

(e) The costs incurred or to be incurred in respect of the transaction can be measured reliably.

However, what constitutes "significant risks" is left to professional judgment.

Expenses associated with revenue (such as cost of goods, along with all associated overhead costs) should be recognized at the same time as revenue within the same transaction. Going by these provisions, you cannot recognize revenue:

a) When the goods sold are still in the seller's warehouse or are to be delivered to the buyer on a future date, even if the buyer has paid for the goods
b) If the buyer has not yet taken possession of the goods, and (in the case of property) if the legal title of ownership of the property has not been transferred to the buyer, except properties acquired through a finance lease.

RENDERING OF SERVICES

When it comes to rendering services, the following recognition criteria apply:

a) The amount of revenue can be measured reliably.
b) It is probable that the economic benefits associated with the transaction will flow to the entity.
c) The stage of completion of the transaction at the balance sheet date can be measured reliably.
d) The costs incurred for the transaction and the costs to complete the transaction can be measured reliably".

While the determination of **cost of sales** (for sales of goods) may be a straightforward affair, the determination of costs incurred for the provision of services may require more effort in the tracking of both the direct and overhead costs associated with the services.

Recognition of revenue for the rendering of services may require the use of the percentage completion method, whereby revenue is recognized based on the percentage of services already rendered. However, the probability of "economic benefits associated with the transaction" flowing to the entity will be higher if the percentage completion recognition criteria are written into the service contract.

In the case of service contracts where an entity receives advance payment to cover a specified number of months for which the expected service is meant to cover, such receipt should first be recognized as Unearned Revenue (a liability). The straight-line method can then be used to recognize revenue arising from the transaction monthly.

INTERESTS, ROYALTIES AND DIVIDENDS

The requirements for the recognition of interests, royalties, and dividends are as follows:

a) Interest shall be recognized using the effective interest method.
b) Royalties shall be recognized on an accrual basis, in accordance with the relevant agreement.
c) Dividends shall be recognized when the shareholder's right to receive payment is established.

TIMING FOR RECOGNITION OF REVENUE & EXPENSE

Timing is very important in the recognition of revenue and expense. Revenues that are not yet due for recognition (such as goods or services paid for but not yet delivered) should be classified as **Unearned Revenue (or Income)**, while expenses arising from goods and services that have not yet satisfied the conditions for recognition (such as goods and services already paid for but not yet received) should be classified as **Prepaid Expense**.

EARNED INCOME

This is the income that has met all the criteria for recognition—sales of goods and services for which all relevant contractual and legal obligations of transferring all the risks of ownership to the buyer have been fulfilled. The accounting entries are as follows:

    Dr.   Cash (or Customer).
    Cr.   Income (Sales).

UNEARNED (DEFERRED) INCOME

Here, we are dealing with income that has not yet met the criteria for recognition. For example, you receive advance payment for goods or services you are yet to deliver or render. For such transactions, you are to recognize Unearned Income—and not income. The following accounting entries apply:

    Dr.   Cash
    Cr.   Unearned Income (Liability)

Unearned Income is a liability account because the money you have collected is not yet yours until you have fulfilled all the necessary contractual or legal obligations. Note that under this system payment for the goods and services may not necessarily coincide with revenue recognition. These are two separate events.

Income Recognition

When the conditions for the recognition of income are met, you will have to derecognize the liability (Unearned Income) and recognize Income by making the following accounting entries:

      Dr.   Unearned Income
      Cr.   Income (Sales)

These entries will convert or transfer Unearned Income to Income.

EXPENSE INCURRED

These are expenses that have met all the criteria for recognition: You have received the goods or services and all the benefits and risks of ownership have been transferred to you. You can go ahead and make the following accounting entries:

      Dr.   Expense
      Cr.   Cash (or Supplier)

PREPAID EXPENSE

This is a situation whereby you have made advance payment for goods or services yet to be delivered or provided in full. Examples include rents and subscriptions payable in advance. You will first have to recognize the payment as a Prepaid Expense, and later recognize the Expense when the conditions for recognition have been met.

<u>Payment</u>

      Dr.   Prepaid Expense (Asset)
      Cr.   Cash

ACCRUED EXPENSE

Accrued expense arises when you have already been provided with goods or services with all the benefits of ownership, but you have yet to pay for them. The accounting entries are similar to the ones above, except for the credit side, where you must substitute the Supplier's account in the place of the Cash account, at the commencement of the contract:

      Dr.   Accrued Expense (Liability)
      Cr.   Supplier

Recognition of Expense

When the conditions for recognition of expense are fully met, you can make the following accounting entries to recognize the expense:

      Dr.   Expense
      Cr.   Prepaid (or Accrued) Expense

The principle of accrued expense sounds like a paradox to me. I will have something more to say on this at the end of this chapter.

    Note that in the case of rent, you will have to recognize the expense based on equal monthly installments until the entire amount is exhausted over the contract period. In the case of goods or services, you may have to use percentage delivery or completion as a basis for the recognition of expense. See worked examples below.

WORKED EXAMPLES ON REVENUE AND EXPENSE RECOGNITION

RENDERING OF SERVICE

EARNED INCOME
These are transactions involving the sale of goods and services which have met all the criteria for the recognition of income. The accounting entries involve immediate recognition of income:

>Dr. Cash/Debtor (Asset)
>Cr. Income

UNEARNED (DEFERRED) INCOME
We have already encountered and defined **unearned income** in this chapter. Let us simply look at a few practical examples here.

Example 1: Service Contract

Consider a 12-month service contract that has been legally executed. Revenue will have to be recognized on a straight-line basis over the twelve months, starting from the date of commencement of the contract, irrespective of the payment terms.

Recognition of Unearned Income

<u>On commencement of contract:</u>
The whole contract sum should be recognized as unearned income:

>Dr. Customer Receivable Account (Asset)
>Cr. Unearned Income (Liability)

Periodic Revenue Recognition
Revenue should be recognized whenever the condition for recognition is met (either by percentage completion or monthly milestone):

>Dr. Unearned Income
>Cr. Revenue (Profit or Loss)

Recognition of Cash Receipt
Whenever the customer makes a payment, either by installment or in full, the following accounting entries should be made:

>Dr. Cash (Asset)
>Cr. Customer Receivable Account

Example 2: Rental Income

Method 1
A property owner received the sum of $1,500 as an advance payment for 1 year from a tenant. The following accounting entries will be applicable (in the book of the property owner):

Recognition of amount received ($1,500) as unearned income
>Dr. Cash/Bank
>Cr. Deferred Revenue

Recognition of monthly rental income of $125
>Dr. Deferred Revenue
>Cr. Revenue—Rent

Method 2
If, on the other hand, the property owner had earlier invoiced the tenant on commencement of the contract before the

receipt of the cash for one year's rent, the following entries would be applicable:

<u>Invoice tenant ($1,500) and recognized unearned income</u>
    Dr. Tenant (Receivable)
    Cr. Deferred Revenue

<u>Recognition of monthly rent as revenue</u>
    Dr. Deferred Revenue
    Cr. Revenue – Rent

<u>On the receipt of cash payment</u>
    Dr. Cash/Bank
    Cr. Tenant (Receivable)

I prefer the second method because it is more representative of accrual accounting. Unearned income should be recognized as soon as there is a valid contractual agreement, irrespective of when payment is made.

SALE OF GOODS

Let us now look at earned and unearned revenue involving sales of goods in the following two cases:
(a) Sale of goods with immediate transfer of ownership, and
(b) Sale of goods with deferred transfer of ownership.

Example 3: Sale of Goods with Immediate Transfer of Ownership
A Trader sold and delivered 100 cell phones to Mr. Adams at $200 per phone. If each phone costs $150, the Trader will have to recognize both the sales revenue and the cost of the phone immediately:

<u>Sales Revenue: ($200 x 100 = $20,000)</u>
    Dr. Cash

        Cr. Sales Revenue

Cost of Goods ($150 x 100 = $15,000)
        Dr. Cost of Goods
        Cr. Inventory

Example 4: Sale of Goods with Deferred Transfer of Ownership

If after Mr. Adams bought the 100 cell phones both Mr. Adams and the Trader agreed that the phones be delivered in batches of 10 per week. Then the Trader will have to recognize both the sales revenue and the cost of goods weekly for 10 weeks (100/10).

Using the same data in Example 3:

a) Cost Price of one phone = $150
b) The Selling Price of one phone = $200

From these, we can compute the following:

1) Total unearned revenue (from 100 phones) = $200 x 100 = $20,000
2) Weekly sales revenue (from 10 delivered phones) = $200 x 10 = $2,000
3) Weekly cost of sale (for 10 delivered phones) = $150 x10 = $1,500

The trader will first recognize unearned revenue of $20,000 arising from the sale of 100 phones (after the agreement):

        Dr. Mr. Adams
        Cr. Unearned Revenue

Every week, after delivering 10 phones, the Trader will recognize both the sales revenue and cost of sale by making the following accounting entries:

Weekly Sale ($2,000)
>   Dr. Unearned Revenue
>   Cr. Revenue

Weekly Cost of Sale ($1,500)
>   Dr. Cost of Goods
>   Cr. Inventory

This will continue until all the phones have been delivered.

Receipt of Payment for the Phones
This is a separate event from income recognition. Receipt of any payment from Mr. Adams for the sale should be acknowledged with the following accounting entries:

>   Dr. Cash/Bank
>   Cr. Mr. Adams

The first purchase did not take cognizance of Mr. Adams' account because it was paid for in cash. However, if Mr. Adams is a regular customer, it is necessary to invoice him before acknowledging the receipt of his payment. If that happens, then the accounting entries will take the following form:

>   After-sale agreement, invoice Mr. Adams for the total sum and recognized unearned income:
>   >   Dr. Mr. Adams (Receivable Account)
>   >   Cr. Unearned Income
>
>   On receipt of payment from Mr. Adams:
>   >   Dr. Cash
>   >   Cr. Mr. Adams Receivable Account

Periodic income recognition continues based on delivery terms.

CUSTOMER LOYALTY PROGRAMME

Many companies, irrespective of size, are employing various means and methods to attract and retain their customers. One such popular method today is the customer loyalty award—an incentive program that rewards customers who meet certain criteria with credits redeemable in the future. The credit is usually redeemed by using it to offset future purchases based on the fair value of the credit.

The **International Financial Reporting Interpretations Committee's Accounting for Customer Loyalty Program (IFRIC 13)** was issued to have a uniform accounting treatment for a practice that is becoming widespread.

Most award credits have expiry dates. All un-redeemed credits should be discharged on expiration.

ACCOUNTING TREATMENT

Before the issuance of IFRC 13, most entities treated the loyalty award credits as marketing expenses, but IFRIC 13 stipulates that the fair value of the award credits should be treated as a separate component of the sale transaction, by allocating it between:

a) The good or service provided
b) The award credits (as Deferred Revenue) to be redeemed in future

Consequently, the following accounting entries become applicable for a **purchase (P)** which results in a **loyalty credit with fair value (X)**:

    Dr.   Cash
                P

Cr.	Sales Revenue	
	P-X	
Cr.	Deferred Revenue (Customer Loyalty)	
	X	

This is similar to the following entries:
- Dr.   Cash
  - P
- Cr.   Sales Revenue
  - P
- Dr.   Customer Loyalty Component of Sales
  - X
- Cr.   Deferred Revenue (Customer Loyalty)
  - X

On redeeming the loyalty credits:
- Dr.   Deferred Revenue (Customer Loyalty)
  - X
- Cr.   Sales Revenue
  - X

On expiration, all expired un-redeemed credits should be released:
- Dr.   Deferred Revenue (Customer Loyalty)
- Cr.   Sales Revenue

If you want to account for Customer Loyalty, make sure you include the relevant account in your Chart of Accounts.

THE PARADOX OF ACCRUED EXPENSE

I have used the term "accrued expense" repeatedly, perhaps, just to fulfill all righteousness. But I have a serious issue with this term. **Accrued Expense** is defined as *expenses that have been incurred but not yet paid for*. Some people have defined it as *"expenses that* have occurred but are not yet recorded through normal processing of transactions..." Whatever the definition, the keyword is **"expenses that have been incurred or that have occurred."**

Why would we choose to record *expenses that have been incurred* as "Accrued Expenses" (which is a liability) instead of just recognizing them as expenses right away? Doesn't this contradict one of the fundamental assumptions of accounting, namely, income and expense should be recognized in the period in which they occurred? Besides, this definition ties payment to the recognition of expense—which is wrong under the accrual basis of accounting. If it is not yet due for recognition, why bother to record it? And if it is due for recognition why defer or accrue it? The **International Financial Reporting Standards (IFRS)** have prescribed the criteria and accounting treatments for **Provisions, Contingent Liabilities, and Contingent Assets** (which are beyond the scope of this book), but **accrued expense** is not considered one of them.

Some definitions of "accrued expense" even go further to say that **"Accrued Expense is the opposite of Prepaid Expense."** This is not true. To see how wrong this is, let us look at the accounting entries that accompany **Prepaid Expense**:

    Dr.   Prepaid Expense (Asset)
    Cr.   Cash

The question is what entries will the beneficiary of this cash payment make in his or her book?
The beneficiary will recognize **Unearned Income** as follows:

    Dr.   Cash
    Cr.   Unearned Income

Thus, we can see that **Unearned Income** (not Accrued Expense) is the mathematical opposite of **Prepaid Expense**.

The general entries for Prepaid Expenses should be:

<u>If payment has already been made:</u>
    Dr. Prepaid Expense (Asset)
    Cr. Cash

<u>If cash is yet to be paid</u>
    Dr. Prepaid Expense (Asset)
    Cr. Supplier

Payment is a separate event from expense recognition, and when payment is made, we must make appropriate entries as follows:

    Dr.   Supplier
    Cr.   Cash

Expense recognition continues, independent of payments, based on contract terms.

This is one good thing about the mathematical approach to accounting: We can always demonstrate the proof, like a mathematical theorem, whenever there is doubt or confusion.

CONSTRUCTION CONTRACTS

Normal revenue and expense recognitions that come under **IAS 18** apply to items of revenue or expense earned and incurred within one accounting period. However, there are cases where items of revenue and expense (or cost) to be accounted for span two or more accounting periods. Accounting for such items will require pro rata recognition of revenue and expense.

WHAT IS A CONSTRUCTION CONTRACT?

When the start and completion dates of revenue (or expense) for an item to be accounted for span reporting periods, then such an item is accounted for as a construction Contract. According to IFRS, a **Construction Contract** is *"a contract specifically negotiated for the construction of an asset or combination of assets that are closely interrelated or independent in terms of their design, technology or function."* The word "construction" can be interpreted to mean build, design, fabricate, create, and develop, thus making it possible to apply **Construction Contract** policies to services such as project management, software development, product marketing, or promotion which could take more than one accounting year to complete. There is a special application of Construction Contracts to the construction of Real Estate.

Construction Contracts can be grouped into a **Fixed-priced contract** (where the contractor agrees to a fixed price or a fixed rate per specified measurable unit) or a **Cost-plus contract** (in which the contractor is reimbursed for all agreed and measurable costs plus a percentage of the costs or a fixed amount). Under both types of contract, a customer can ask for a **variation** in the scope of work to be done (which may affect the cost of the contract either positively or negatively), and the contractor can make **claims** for an additional amount for cost not included in the original contract. Sometimes, a Construction Contract may include an option for **incentive payment** to the contractor if a specified standard or job completion date is met.

IAS 11 prescribes the criteria for the recognition of revenue and cost arising from Construction Contracts. It prescribes the rules on how to allocate revenue and cost to the accounting periods in which the construction occurred. Note that the Standard only applies to accounting in the financial statements of *contractors*; what happens at the customer's side of the transaction will depend on the type of asset being constructed or created.

CONTRACT REVENUE AND COST

Contract revenues comprise the **initial contract price** plus all subsequent **variations**, **claims,** and **incentives**, while contract costs comprise the following:

a) Direct cost (such as cost of materials, labor, depreciation on equipment, equipment hiring cost, etc.)
b) General contract overhead cost (such as warranty or insurance cost, cost for the transportation of materials, and any overhead cost attributable to the contract)

c) Other costs (costs that are chargeable to the customer under the terms of the contract such as compensations and other claims from third parties).

Note that the recognition criteria for all aspects of revenues and cost arising from the Construction Contract must satisfy part of **IAS 18** requirements for the recognition of revenue and cost, namely, reliable measurement of revenue and cost. If it cannot be measured, then it cannot be recognized.

One contentious issue is whether the cost incurred in the process of securing the contract should be included in the contract cost. Going by the provisions of the Standard, such costs can only be included if they can be reliably measured, and it is probable that the contract will be secured within the reporting period. However, if those pre-contract costs have already been expended, then they cannot be reallocated to the contract no matter the circumstance.

Having identified what constitutes contract revenue and costs, let us briefly look at those items that are not recognized as costs under the Construction Contract. They include:

1) Selling and marketing cost
2) General and administrative costs not specifically provided for reimbursement in the contract
3) Non-reimbursable research and development cost
4) Depreciations on plant and machinery not directly used in the execution of the contract.

Recognition of Contract Revenue and Expenses

IAS 11 provides the following criteria for the recognition of contract revenue and expenses in the income statement:

a) Revenue and costs associated with a construction contract can only be recognized when the outcome of the contract can be reliably measured
b) Revenue and expenses shall be recognized by reference to the stage of completion of the contract activity at the balance sheet date

When can a reliable estimate be determined for the *outcome* of a construction contract? The first criterion is the general requirement of IAS 18 (Revenue): **when it is probable that the economic benefit of the contract will flow to the entity**. The following additional requirements apply for a ***fixed-price*** contract:

1) Reliable measurement of total contract revenue
2) Reliable estimate of both the cost to complete the contract, as well as the stage of completion on the balance sheet date.

For a ***cost-plus*** contract, the only additional requirement is the identification and reliable measurement of all costs attributable to the contract whether specifically reimbursable or not.

Contract revenue and expenses are recognized based on the ***percentage-of-completion method***, which involves matching revenue with costs incurred for the actual work done in reaching a specific completion stage. This is the only method permitted under IAS 11 for the recognition of contract revenues and expenses. The method, whereby contract revenue and expenses are recognized only after completion of contract (completed-contract method), is not allowed under IFRS.

In an event where it becomes likely that contract costs will exceed contract revenue, then the loss should be recognized immediately in the income statement irrespective of the stage of completion.

DETERMINATION OF PERCENTAGE OF COMPLETION

Reliable measurement of the stages of completion of a construction contract is very crucial for accurate determination of revenue and expenses to be recognized. Where a contract provides measurable job completion milestones as the basis for stages of completion, such milestones can be used as a basis for the recognition of contract revenue and expenses. Where such milestones do not exist, IAS 11 provides the following methods for the estimation of percentage completion for a contract, depending on the nature of the contract:

a) The proportion of costs method matches the portion of cost incurred against the total contract cost and recognizes revenue based on the percentage of total cost incurred against the total costs required to complete the contract. For example, if the total cost required to complete a forty thousand Dollar contract is twenty thousand Dollars, and if the total cost incurred as of the reporting date is five thousand Dollars, then the percentage of completion (which is 20%) can be computed as follows:

Total Contract Revenue		$40,000
Total Contract Cost		$20,000
Total Cost incurred (as of reporting date)		$5,000

Percentage Completion	(5,000/20,000) x 100	20%
Contract Revenue to be recognized (20% of total revenue) for the period	(20/100) *400,000	$80,000

b) Independent surveys and physical verification of the value of the actual work done can also be used to determine the percentage of work completed.

CONTRACT WORK IN PROGRESS

In many situations, it is advantageous to buy construction materials in bulk (more than the actual quantity required at a given moment) and deliver the materials to the site to take advantage of volume discounts or future unfavorable price fluctuations. Costs for the portion of materials not yet used (those meant for future use) should be recognized as assets and classified under Contract Work in Progress. This cost should not be included in the total cost used for the computation of percentage completion for revenue recognition.

Note that the actual amount received for the contract is not equal to the amount recognized as revenue, as some receipts may include **advances**. All advances should be recognized as a **liability due to customers**. The total amount billed to the customer for contract work carried out (whether paid or unpaid) called **Progress billings**, should be recognized as an **asset due from the customer**. Some contracts may provide for **retention**—part of the contract amount that is withheld until certain conditions are met.

DISCLOSURE

The following disclosures, most of which are expected on the face of the financial statements, should form part of your financial statements or notes:

a) The amount of contract revenue recognized as revenue during the period should be disclosed in the Statement of Comprehensive Income, and the method used for revenue recognition and stage of completion should form part of the accounting policies disclosure.
b) The following disclosures are required in the Statement of Financial Position: total advances received, the amount held as retention, total amount due to customer, total amount due from customer, and contract work in progress. Contingent assets and liabilities such as warranty and claims (in accordance with the relevant Standards) should also be disclosed.

INVENTORIES

Many businesses stock goods either for sale or as raw materials for the production of goods or the provision of services for sale. The major accounting issues here involve the appropriate calculation of cost and the recognition of revenue and expenses associated with sales. One additional issue here is the **inventory write-down** operations. We will examine these and other issues in this chapter.

BASIC DEFINITIONS AND RECOGNITION OF INVENTORY

WHAT IS INVENTORY?

Inventories are assets that are:

a) Held as raw materials to be used in the production of goods or provision of services.
b) In the process of being transformed into goods (also called Work-in-progress).
c) In the form of finished products or goods held for sale in the ordinary course of business.

A manufacturing entity starts by building a raw materials inventory and later transfers the materials to Work-in progress inventory before coming out with the finished products inventory. But a retail trader who simply buys goods for resale does not need this transformation.

INVENTORY COST

Inventory costs comprise the following:

a) Cost of purchase (including taxes, import duties, transportation and handling charges, etc.).
b) Production or conversion cost which includes all direct costs and overhead costs attributable to converting the raw materials to finished goods.

The following costs are excluded:

a) Raw materials waste
b) Non-production storage costs
c) Overhead costs not directly attributable to the production of the item
d) Selling costs such as advertising and promotion

Cost accounting is a major topic in accounting and is beyond the scope of this book.

NET REALIZABLE VALUE (NRV)

Net Realizable Value (NRV) is the **estimated selling price** less the **total estimated transaction costs**.

MEASUREMENT OF INVENTORY COST

Inventories are measured or valued at the lower of **Cost** or **Net Realizable Value**.

INVENTORY COSTS AND COSTING METHODS

When inventory items have uniform properties and are interchangeable, one of the following methods can be used to determine the cost of individual items as new items are added to the inventory:

a) **First-In-First-Out (FIFO)**
b) **Weighted average**

In **FIFO**, it is assumed that items are sold according to the order in which they were purchased or produced (from first to last). The **weighted average** costing method recomputes a new cost for each item whenever new items are added by computing the weighted average of the new and old items.

If, for example, there were 100 items, with a unit cost of $250, before the arrival of a new batch of 50 new units of the same items, costing $225 each, under FIFO it is assumed that the 100 items that were originally in stock will be sold before the 50 new items. But using the weighted average method the new cost for each of the 150 items can be computed as follows:

$$\text{Cost} = \frac{100 \times 250 + 50 \times 225}{100 + 50} = 241.67$$

These two are the only cost measurement methods allowed under IFRS. Other measurement methods, such as Last-In-First-Out (LIFO) are not permitted.

INVENTORIES WRITE-DOWN

Under IFRS, it is strictly recommended that assets should not be carried at amounts likely to be higher than their sale or fair values. This is to ensure that "toxic" assets are eliminated from the book instead of using such assets as camouflage to deceive investors.

There are many situations which can impact negatively on the carrying value of assets, and they include:

a) Damages
b) Obsolescence
c) Decline in selling price

Whenever any of these events becomes obvious it is necessary to write down the value of the inventory to its net realizable value (NRV). The write-down is carried out on a per-item basis.

All losses incurred because of inventory write-down should be recognized as expenses in the period in which the write-down occurred. *Write-down* loss can be reversed if the condition later becomes favorable. Any amount incurred because of reversal should be recognized as a reduction in the loss recorded for the previous write-down within the same period.

Write-down estimates must reflect the purpose for which the inventories are held. For example, inventories that are held for sale should be *written down* against the prevailing market prices, but inventories that are held for servicing sales contracts should be written down against contract prices. You may require the services of an expert to write down inventories in the absence of good software.

STANDARD ACCOUNTING ENTRIES ASSOCIATED WITH INVENTORY

SALES

When inventories are sold revenue is recognized along with the related cost simultaneously. The accounting entries are as follows:

Selling Price

Dr. Cash/Debtor
Cr. Sales Revenue

Cost Price
Dr. Cost of Sales (Expense)
Cr. Inventory

PURCHASES

Cost Price
Dr. Inventory
Cr. Cash/Creditor

Remember to re-compute the cost price of each item using any of the two recommended costing methods.

WRITE-DOWN

Write-down Losses
Dr. Inventory Write-down Loss (Profit or Loss)
Cr. Inventory

WRITE-DOWN REVERSAL

Write-down Gains
Dr. Inventory
Cr. Inventory Write-down Loss (Profit or Loss)

TRANSFERS

In a production process, raw materials are transferred to work-in-progress and from work-in-progress to finished goods, before they are sold. All such transfers are carried out at cost:

  Cost
  Dr. Target or Destination Inventory
  Cr. Source Inventory

MANUAL INVENTORY UPDATES

Apart from sales and purchases, which update the inventory directly, it might be necessary to manually adjust inventory due to several reasons. One good example is when some items are damaged or have expired. Such items must be manually removed from stock, followed by journal entries. In this situation, both the *Inventory Register* and inventory movement (*Inventory Journal*) must be updated manually. However, for the General Ledger entries, the items must be written off at cost with the following entries:

  Dr. Cost of Sales (or Inventory Write-off Expense)
  Cr. Inventory

THE INVENTORY REGISTER

Irrespective of whether you are managing your inventory manually or with an automated system, a good inventory register is a must. While the accounting entries are posted to the General Ledger, your inventory register must keep accurate details of the quantity of each item in stock, as well as the *in* and *out* movements of each item.

 The basic data fields required in the inventory register are as follows:

 a) Item Code (unique for each item)
 b) Item Description

c) Item Class or Category
d) Unit Cost Price
e) Unit Selling Price
f) Unit of Measure
g) Quantity in Stock
h) Re-order Quantity.
i) ...
j) Inventory Account Code
k) Sales Account Code
l) Cost of Sales Account Code
m) ...
n) Last Update Date

There may be a need for additional fields, depending on the implementation, but these are just the basic ones. It is important to group items into defined classes or categories in the register, and associate each item to existing inventory, sale, and cost of sale accounts in the chart of accounts.

ACCOUNTING FOR SALARY & WAGES

Processing and paying employees' salaries are rituals all entities—whether big or small—go through, at least, once a month. The issue here is not just about preparing and paying salary, it also involves making proper and accurate accounting entries to reflect all the earnings and deductions arising from employees' salary. Whether you are preparing salary manually or with payroll software, the issues I am going to discuss here apply. But you will find things more convenient if you have payroll software that is integrated with accounting software for direct updates. In the absence of such software, you will have to rely on manual journal entries.

Salary structures vary from jurisdiction to jurisdiction and from entity to entity, but for this discussion, we shall adopt a generic salary structure shown below:

Earnings

a) Basic Salary
b) Housing
c) Transport
d) Entertainment
e) Other Allowances
f) Bonus
g) Overtime

h) Other Earnings

Deductions

a) Payroll Tax (PAYE)
b) Pension
c) Loan
d) Cooperative
e) Other Deductions

PAYROLL ACCOUNTING METHODS

Before we go into the issue of accounting entries, let us examine those accounts we must have in the chart of accounts. They include:

1) **Payroll Clearing (or Control)** account—a liability account used as a temporary account after preparing salary (before the actual payment)
2) **Salary Expense**—expense accounts for different categories of earnings
3) **Payroll Liability**—accounts for each category of deduction

In particular, the following accounts should be created for Pension:

a) **Employees' Pension Liability**, which is to be credited with the total (combined employees' and employer's) pension contributions.
b) **Employer's Pension Expense** which is to be debited with the employer's part of the contribution. We will see later where the credit part of the employees' contributions goes.

ACCOUNTING FOR EARNINGS

After preparing the salary for each month (before making the actual payment), the following accounting entries should be made:

> Dr. Salary Expense
> Cr. Payroll Clearing Account

Some entities choose to charge all earnings into one account called **salary & wages**. While this might be okay for convenience, it does not allow you to account for each component of salary expense.

ACCOUNTING FOR DEDUCTIONS

All deductions are from employees' earned income. Most of these deductions are liabilities (except internal loans deduction) which the company will later remit to the appropriate authorities.

Generally, each deduction requires the following accounting entries:

> Dr. Payroll Liability
> Cr. Payroll Clearing Account

Let us examine the accounting treatment for some of the special payroll deductions:

Payroll Tax

Payroll Tax, also called PAYE (Pay-As-You-Earn) in some jurisdictions, is a deduction from each employee's salary which the employer is expected to remit to the government. It is a liability to be cleared after remitting the money to the appropriate authority. Make sure you have a unique Payroll Tax Liability account in your chart of accounts.

After preparing salary:
>Dr. Payroll Clearing account
>Cr. Payroll Tax Liability

After remitting the tax:
>Dr. Payroll Tax Liability
>Cr. Bank/Cash

Pension

This is another liability on the part of the employer. Pension administration may vary from country to country. In some jurisdictions, Employees' Pension comprises two components:

a) Employee's contribution
b) Employer's Contribution

It is the total of these two components that are remitted to the government or its agency. However, only the employee part is fully accounted for as part of the salary, a separate journal entry may be required to complete the employer's part of the contributions. The employer part of the contribution is written off as an expense.

After preparing salary, the following accounting entries should be made:

>Dr. Payroll Control Account (Employees' Contributions)
>Dr. Pension Expense (Employer's Contributions)
>Cr. Pension Liability (Total Contributions)

After remitting the Pension:
>Dr. Pension Liability account
>Cr. Bank/Cash account

Note that the last entries should be made through your accounting system. They are not part of the payroll.

Loans

Granting loans to employees is what many entities in some countries do. Often these interest-free loans are repaid by deducting fixed amounts from employees' salary every month.

Before we can treat the monthly loan deductions from employees' salaries, we need to refer back to when the loan was given to the employee. Each employee should have a unique account under the current asset group, EMPLOYEE LOANS AND ADVANCES. This account should be **debited with the total amount the employee is loaned**, while Cash or Bank account is credited.

After granting the loan:
   Dr. Employee's Loan account
   Cr. Cash/Bank

Each month the employee repays the loan (through a deduction from salary):
   Dr. Payroll Control account
   Cr. Employee's Loan account

This must be continued until the loan is fully repaid.

PREPARING AND PAYING SALARY

After preparing salary, all earnings go to the credit side of the Payroll Clearing account, while all deductions go to the debit side. The balance in this account (Credit-Debit) is the net salary. This account will have to be cleared after paying the salary either by issuing cash to the employees or remitting the salary to the bank. Below is the summary of the accounting entries:

After Preparing Salary:

   Earnings
   Dr. Salary Expense.

Cr. Payroll Clearing Account (Gross Earning).

Deductions
Dr. Payroll Clearing Account (Total Deductions).
Cr. Relevant payroll liability account (as discussed above).

After Paying Salary:
Dr. Payroll Clearing Account (Net Pay).
Cr. Cash or Bank (Net Pay).

These last entries complete the general processes of preparing and paying employees' salaries. However, variations may exist in different countries and jurisdictions.

ACCRUED SALARY

One of the numerous challenges small business owners face includes paying themselves salary as when due, along with other employees. This can be attributed to insufficient funds or the absence of a good accounting culture. Whatever the case, you will still have to prepare your salary as described above and recognize all the expenses and liabilities, whether there is money to pay everybody or not. Actual payment can always be made when money is available.

To account for the Directors' unpaid salary, you will create a liability account called ACCRUED DIRECTOR'S SALARY and make the following accounting entries from your accounting system for each month the salary is not paid:

After preparing salary:
Dr. Salary Expense
Cr. Accrued Director's Salary

Whenever the director receives his or her salary:
Dr. Accrued Director's Salary

Cr. Cash/Bank

Generally, payroll expenses and liabilities should be recognized in the period in which they occur, irrespective of whether there is money to pay the salary or not. What this means is always prepare the salary on or before the end of the month whether there is money to pay the salary or not. Recognition of expense is a separate event from the payment of cash. This complies with the IFRS requirement for the accrual recognition of expenses.

SUMMARY OF ACCOUNTS REQUIRED FOR PAYROLL

Below are the various accounts required for Payroll accounting:

Personnel Expense (Profit or Loss)
1) Basic Salary
2) Housing Allowance
3) Transport Allowance
4) Entertainment Allowance
5) Other Allowances
6) Overtime
7) Bonus
8) Other Personnel Cost
9) Employer's Pension Expense

Payroll Liabilities
1) PAYE Tax
2) Pension
3) Staff Cooperative
4) Other Payroll Liabilities
5) Payroll Clearing Account

Payroll Assets
1) Each Employee's Loan Repayment Account.

Loan deductions are not quite assets, but reductions in employees' liabilities to the company.

Note
Whether you use the term **Personnel Cost** or **Personnel Expense** depends on the accounting structure and costing mechanism of the organization. Service companies that bill their clients based on man-hours classify salary as Personnel Cost, otherwise, it should be classified as Expense.

TAXES

Tax is as old as man. It has been one of the primary motives for feudal wars, the historic quest for conquests, expansion of empires and kingdoms. It was (and is still) the insignia of authority and power, as a state cannot qualify as such without drawing some form of tax from the people within its domain. This is how Adam Smith (1723-90) the great economist, in his *The Wealth of Nations*, put it: "There is no art which one government sooner learns of another than that of draining money from the pockets of the people."

Because of the importance of tax and its implications, I have decided to devote this chapter to some basic accounting treatments for taxes. I have decided to focus a little more attention on **Withholding Tax** and **Value-Added Tax (VAT)** because of their prevalence in many jurisdictions.

TYPES OF TAXES

Most taxes are statutory—their administrations are governed by enabling legislation. It is not possible to list all the various forms of taxes available in all jurisdictions throughout the world, but I will just mention a few here before going ahead to provide the general accounting entries for taxes.

Personal Income Tax or Payroll Tax

This is the statutory tax every citizen is expected to pay. For those in paid employment, the tax is deducted by their employers and remitted to the government. Those not in paid employment are taxed by direct assessment through the declaration of their income for the period under consideration. We have already dealt with the accounting treatments for payroll tax in the previous chapter.

Company Income Tax

This is the tax profit-oriented companies are required to pay to the government. It is usually a fixed percentage of the company's profit for the period under consideration. The rate varies from country to country, ranging from very low to very high.

Capital Gains Tax

Capital Gain Tax is the tax imposed on profits arising from the sale of assets.

Stamp Duty

This is the tax paid for some transactions which involve obtaining certain documents from the government. The definition and scope of Stamp Duty Tax may be very wide in some jurisdictions.

Others include **Withholding Tax** and **Value-Added Tax**. We are going to take a more detailed look at these two in subsequent sections.

GENERAL ACCOUNTING ENTRIES FOR TAX

Often, companies collect taxes on behalf of the government before remitting such monies to appropriate government agencies. Thus, entities involved in tax collections will have to account both for collections and remittances.

When tax is collected, the following accounting entries must be made:
    Dr.   Cash
    Cr.   Tax Payables (Liability)

When the money is remitted to the government:
    Dr.   Tax Payables
    Cr.   Cash

ACCOUNTING FOR WITHHOLDING TAX

Withholding tax is the amount withheld as a tax on earned income from either individuals or organizations. Withholding tax is also referred to as **retention tax** in some jurisdictions, and its administration differs from jurisdiction to jurisdiction.

In some countries, withholding tax deducted from a company's income is a retention that will be used to offset the company's income tax when tax returns are officially filed. If the final tax due is less than the total amount withheld, then the difference is refunded, otherwise the entity pays the balance to the government. If no returns are made, the money remains with the government.

There are two types of withholding tax:

1) **Withholding Tax Payable**, which is the withholding tax an entity deducts from suppliers' income on behalf of the government. This is a liability in the book of the collector.
2) **Withholding Tax Receivable**, which is the withholding tax deducted from your income either by the government or an entity acting on behalf of the government. This will appear as an asset in your book. Always demand a certificate after every such deduction.

Withholding Tax Payable is remitted to the government after deduction while Withholding Tax Receivable is used to offset actual income tax.

The withholding Tax rate is either determined by the tax authorities or fixed by legislation. In some jurisdictions, the supply of goods attracts a lower rate of withholding tax than the provision of services.

ACCOUNTING ENTRIES FOR WITHHOLDING TAX

Below are the standard accounting entries for Withholding Tax.

When you deduct withholding tax from suppliers:
    Dr.   Cash
    Cr.   Withholding Tax Payable (Liability)

When withholding tax is deducted from your cash receipts:
    Dr.   Withholding Tax Receivable (Asset)
    Cr.   Cash/Bank

When you remit Withholding Tax to the government:
    Dr.   Withholding Tax Payable
    Cr.   Cash/Bank

After filing your Income Tax returns with the government:

A. Assuming your Income Tax (**T**) is higher than your Withholding Tax Receivable (**W**) with a difference of (**D**), you will make the following accounting entries:

Dr. Income Tax Expense (with **T**)
Cr. Withholding Tax Payable (with **W**)
Cr. Cash/Bank (with **D**)

D represents the additional tax you will pay to the government.

B. If, on the other hand, your Income Tax (**T**) is less than your Withholding Tax Receivable (**W**) with a difference of (**D**), you will make the following accounting entries (D represents the balance the government will refund to you. But trust governments, they are not likely to refund the difference immediately):

    Dr.   Income Tax Expense (with **T**)
    Cr.   Withholding Tax Payable (with **T**)

These entries will leave your Withholding Tax Receivable account with a debit balance of D (W-T), pending when a refund is made to you. When the difference is finally refunded to you, then you can make the following accounting entries:

    Dr.   Cash (with **D**)
    Cr.   Withholding Tax Payable (with **D**)

This will clear the account and close the transaction.

One thing you can do to enhance your understanding of this topic is to substitute actual figures for T, W, and D and see how the entries line up.

ACCOUNTING FOR VALUE-ADDED TAX (VAT)

VAT is a form of consumption tax imposed on selected goods and services. Some goods and services (such as drugs, medical equipment, books, educational materials, and services) are exempted from Value-Added Tax.

VAT rate varies from jurisdiction to jurisdiction and is usually fixed by legislation. Some countries do not charge VAT, but they may have other forms of taxes (such as Sales Tax) similar to VAT.

CLASSIFICATION OF VALUE-ADDED TAX

Output VAT

Output VAT (or **VAT Payable**) refers to the VAT you collect from others for the goods and services you sell to them. It is a liability that must be offset by remitting the money collected to the government. Output VAT account should be set up as a liability under Other Payables in your chart of accounts.

Input VAT

Input VAT (or **VAT Receivable**) is the VAT you pay on goods you purchase from others for resale. Input VAT is refundable, as it is used to offset Output VAT. What you are expected to remit to the government is an excess of Output VAT over Input VAT. Input VAT account should be set up as an asset under Other Receivables in your chart of accounts.

VAT Expense

VAT paid on overhead, general, and administrative expenses is non-refundable. They are written off as expenses.

ACCOUNTING ENTRIES FOR VALUE-ADDED TAX

The following accounting entries apply to the various classes of VAT mentioned above. Note that the accounting entries only involve the VAT component.

VAT Payable or Output VAT
      Dr.   Cash or Customer

        Cr.   VAT Payable

VAT Receivable or Input VAT
        Dr.   VAT Receivable
        Cr.   Cash or Supplier

VAT Expense
        Dr.   VAT Expense
        Cr.   Cash or Supplier

VAT Set Off

The easiest way to prepare your monthly VAT Returns is to create a VAT control account and use it as a clearing account for VAT payments and receipts. At the end of every reporting period, make the following accounting entries:

<u>With Total VAT Payable (Output VAT)</u>
        Dr.   VAT Payable (Output) Account.
        Cr.   VAT Clearing Account.
<u>With Total VAT Receivable (Input VAT)</u>
        Dr.   VAT Clearing Account.
        Cr.   VAT Receivable (Input) Account.

Note that you will also have to treat **VAT Taken at Source** as VAT Receivable (see note below).

VAT Payment
VAT is remitted monthly in arrears, and the remittable amount is the excess of VAT Payable over VAT Receivable (the Balance in the VAT Clearing Account).

The following accounting entries apply to VAT remittance.

<u>If Output VAT is greater than Input VAT</u>

Dr. VAT Clearing Account
Cr. Cash/Bank (Amount remitted)

VAT Receipt
When your VAT Input is greater than your VAT Output, you are entitled to a cash receipt. Based on the set of entries earlier made, the following accounting entries apply to VAT receipts:

If Input VAT is greater than Output VAT
Dr. Cash/Bank (Amount received)
Cr. VAT Clearing Account

VAT Taken at Source
Some entities and agencies of government have been mandated to deduct VAT at source from their suppliers and vendors and make returns to the government. What this means is instead of the VAT you include in your invoice being paid to you it is deducted. You are expected to report this type of VAT separately so that it can be offset against your Output VAT. However, you will need to obtain a certificate from your customer as evidence for VAT taken at source. VAT Taken at Source should be set up as an asset in your chart of accounts and debited with the amount deducted.

Practical Example:

Let us consider a transaction where you invoice your customer the sum of $5000, along with a 5% VAT. The VAT on this invoice amounts to $250, giving a total of $5,250 for the whole invoice. This is what you expect your customer to pay you under normal circumstances. However, if your customer is one of those agencies of government mandated to deduct VAT at source, you will receive $5,000 only.

In addition to VAT, your customer may also decide to deduct a withholding tax of, say 5%, from your payment. If that happens, you will receive the sum of $4500 ($5000-5% 0f $5000).

The standard accounting entries for VAT taken at source are as follows:

<u>If VAT only is deducted</u>:
      Dr.   Cash/Bank (Invoice amount - VAT)
      Cr.   Customer (Invoice amount + VAT)
      Dr.   VAT Taken at Source (VAT)

<u>If Withholding Tax (WHT) is also deducted in addition to the VAT</u>:
      Dr.   Cash/Bank (Invoice amount - VAT - WHT)
      Cr.   Customer (Invoice amount + VAT)
      Dr.   VAT Taken at Source (VAT)
      Dr.   Withholding Tax (WHT)

Note:
As part of your VAT returns, you are expected to disclose the following types of VAT separately (in addition to VAT Output and Input) in some jurisdictions:

a) VAT on Imports.
b) VAT that is taken at source on behalf of the government by agents of government during payments.
c) VAT Expense (for non-refundable VAT).

Good accounting software should be able to automate some or all of these. Whatever you are using, just make sure that you set up all the relevant VAT accounts to capture each category of VAT.

PROPERTY, PLANT AND EQUIPMENT (FIXED ASSETS)

Acquiring tangible assets is a normal practice every organization is very familiar with. But what most people don't seem to be aware of are the accounting treatments that must accompany each of the assets. You may have come across the term "toxic assets." It is one of the results of improper accounting for tangible assets.

In Chapter 1, we discussed the classification of assets into Current and Noncurrent categories. However, the International Financial Reporting Standards IFRS) has provided a new category called Noncurrent Assets for all tangible and intangible assets. Some of the items in the class include:

a) Property, Plant, and Equipment
b) Intangible Assets
c) Investment Property
d) Noncurrent Assets Held for Sale
e) Biological Assets

In this chapter, we will be dealing with **Property, Plant, and Equipment (PPE)**—what was generally referred to as **Fixed Assets** under GAAP. I may be using the names **Fixed Assets** and **Property, Plant and Equipment** interchangeably.

IAS 16 is the Standard that prescribes the rules for the recognition, initial and subsequent measurements, as well as the disclosure requirements for Property, Plant, and Equipment. IAS 16 does not cover those items already accounted for by other Standards, such as:

a) Investment Property
b) Noncurrent Assets Held for Sale (IFRS 5)
c) Biological agricultural assets (IAS 41)
d) Evaluation of mineral rights and reserves (IFRS 6)

DEFINITION AND RECOGNITION CRITERIA

Property, Plant, and Equipment (PPE) can be defined as *"tangible assets that are held for use in production or supply of goods and services, for rentals or administrative purposes"* and are expected to be used for more than one accounting period.

The recognition criteria for PPE are as follows:

a) It is probable that future economic benefits embodied in the asset will flow into the entity controlling the asset.
b) The cost of the asset can be reliably measured.

Below are the definitions of some of the key terms associated with Property, Plant, and Equipment.

ASSET COST

This is the total amount paid to acquire or construct the asset. Asset cost comprises of the following:

a) Purchase price (including taxes, import duties, discounts, etc.)

b) Transportation, handling, and other charges incurred in the process of bringing the asset to the location where it will be used
c) Installation, set up, and other costs directly attributable to bringing the asset to the state whereby it can be used as intended

The following costs are excluded:

a) Operational and administrative overhead costs not directly attributable to the acquisition of the asset
b) Advertising and promotional costs
c) Training costs

USEFUL LIFE

This is the length of time the asset is expected to be used (usually in years) or some production units expected from the use of the asset.

RESIDUAL VALUE

This is the estimated disposal (sale) amount, minus the cost to sell, of the asset at the end of its useful life.

DEPRECIABLE AMOUNT

This is the cost of the asset less its residual value. This is the amount that is depreciated:

Depreciable Amount = Asset Cost – Residual Value

DEPRECIATION

This is the periodic allocation of wears and tears on the asset as cost to the expense account over the useful life of the asset. This allocation could be on a monthly or yearly basis. The sum of all the depreciation up to any given time is called **accumulated depreciation**.

Sometimes, depreciation is specified by the yearly **depreciation rate**, which is a constant value representing the percentage of the depreciable amount to be charged as depreciation expense.

One important issue about depreciation is the method of depreciation used. Some of the permitted methods include the **straight-line**, **reducing-balance,** and **sum-of-the-year's digits**. The **straight-line** method of depreciation, which apportions depreciation equally over each year (or each production unit) of the asset's service life, remains the most common.

Entities are free to select any method of depreciation, but any method selected must match the pattern of usage or consumption of the item. The same method must be used for all the items within the same class. Note that IFRS prohibits the selection of accounting policies based on tax considerations. This also applies to the selection of the depreciation method.

CARRYING AMOUNT

The **carrying amount** of an asset, also called **net book value** (NBV), is the asset **cost** less **accumulated depreciation** (and impairment losses—if any):

> **Carrying Amount = Cost − Accumulated Depreciation − Impairment Loss**

FAIR VALUE

This is the amount at which the asset can be sold or exchanged between knowledgeable and willing parties in a formal, neutral, and unbiased transaction. Fair value reflects the true value of the asset.

RECOVERABLE AMOUNT

This is the asset's **net selling price** or its **value in use**—whichever is higher.

IMPAIRMENT

Impairment loss is the amount by which the carrying amount of an asset exceeds its recoverable amount. Impairment of assets is extensively covered under a separate Standard known as IAS 36.

MEASUREMENTS POLICY

INITIAL MEASUREMENT

On recognition, an item of PPE shall be measured at the total of what it costs to acquire the asset. The following accounting entries apply on initial recognition:

      Dr.   Asset Cost
      Cr.   Cash/Creditor

At this point, accumulated depreciation is zero. However, the **Depreciable Amount** is computed as *Asset Cost – Residual Value.*

SUBSEQUENT MEASUREMENTS

For subsequent measurements, there are two models to choose from: **Cost** or **Revaluation** model.

Cost Model

The **Cost** model (also called **depreciation model**) involves the systematic apportionment of a specified amount (based on the depreciation method used) representing a part of the original cost as depreciation expense over the life of the asset, using a known depreciation method.

The following accounting entries apply to the cost model:

Depreciation
      Dr.   Depreciation Expense A/C
      Cr.   Accumulated Depreciation A/C

After depreciation, the **carrying amount** of each asset, measured under the cost model, must be recomputed as follows:

Carrying Amount = Asset Cost − Accumulated Depreciation

Revaluation Model

The revaluation method requires physical revaluation of the asset (or class of assets) at regular intervals to obtain a new value for the asset based on its fair values. Any gain arising from revaluation should be recognized in Other Comprehensive Income (Equity) under the heading "Revaluation Surplus" while losses should be recognized as an expense in Profit or Loss.

Below is the summary of accounting entries for revaluation gain or loss:

Gain: Carrying Amount - Revalued Amount > 0
      Dr.   Asset Cost A/C.

Cr. Revaluation Surplus (Other Comprehensive Income under Equity).

A reversal of an earlier increase for the same asset should be debited to *Other Comprehensive Income*.

Loss: Carrying Amount - Revalued Amount < 0 or
Revalued Amount – Carrying Amount > 0

Dr. Revaluation Loss (Profit or Loss) A/C
Cr. Asset Cost A/C

A reversal of an earlier loss for the same asset should be credited to *Profit or Loss*.

Note:
A revaluation surplus may be released to Retained Earnings when the asset is derecognized or disposed of. On no account should a revaluation surplus be credited to Profit or Loss.

COMPONENTIZATION

Componentization policy simply states, *component parts of an item of property, plant and equipment with different useful lives or depreciation rates and with costs that are significant, in relation to the total cost, must be depreciated separately*. However, what is considered "significant" is left to judgment (some jurisdictions may consider anything from 5% as being significant).

Componentization is one challenging issue for entities converting from GAAP to IFRS, as there may be no sufficient data for the componentization of existing assets.

CHANGES IN ESTIMATES

IFRS requires an annual review of the **useful lives, residual values,** and **depreciation methods** of items of property, plants, and equipment, and the estimates are adjusted whenever necessary based on prevailing realities and circumstances. For example, the residual value of an item can be adjusted upward if existing market indicators suggest so. These adjustments are regarded as changes in estimates and do not warrant any accounting entry since they are not corrections of errors. However, they will affect the *carrying amount* of the asset in the current and future periods only.

IMPAIRMENTS

An impairment loss is defined as *the amount by which the carrying amount of an asset exceeds its recoverable amount* (*recoverable amount* is the higher of net selling price and value in use).
Yearly impairment testing is mandatory for some classes of assets. You are expected to collate a yearly schedule of impairment losses and make appropriate adjustments to assets carrying values and depreciation charges based on these losses. Provision should also be made for the reversal of impairment losses (except for *Goodwill*) and the readjustment of the carrying values and depreciation charges for the affected assets.

The following accounting entries apply to impairment loss:
   Dr.   Impairment Loss (Profit or Loss)
   Cr.   Asset Cost

COMPONENT REPLACEMENT OR UPGRADE

Routine repairs and maintenance costs for items of property, plant, and equipment are written off as expenses. However, when a major component of the asset involving a significant cost is replaced then the cost can be capitalized. Such capitalization can only be allowed under the following conditions: **if the cost of the replaced component was separately identified on initial recognition and it is evident that the replacement will result in more economic benefits.**

If there is no data to determine the cost of the replaced component, then the replacement cost can be used to determine the initial cost of the replaced component by discounting it back to its present value at the time of initial recognition. This value must be taken out of the book before adding the cost of the replaced component.

Replacing the engine of a car will result in more economic benefits, at least in terms of performance and reduction in repairs and maintenance costs. However, the cost of the engine and the chassis of a car are not usually quoted separately on purchase. However, the cost of replacing the engine meets the requirement for capitalization.

Assuming the car was bought for $40,000 five years ago, and the cost of the replaced engine is $5,000. Using the appropriate discounting rate, we can determine the approximate cost of the engine five years ago, when the car was bought, through its Present Value (P) using the formula:

$$P = \frac{A}{(1+i)^n}$$

(where **A** is the future amount, **i** *is* the discount rate, and **n** is the number of years).

Based on the above formula, (if we take 10% as the discount rate) the cost of the engine five years ago when the car was initially purchased can be computed as **$5,000/(1+0.1)^5 = $3,105.59**.

This amount must be taken out of the book through the following accounting entries:

Discounted Cost of the Engine ($3,105.59)
- Dr. Accumulated Depreciation.
- Cr. Asset Cost.

The cost of the new component ($5,000) should be added to the book, by passing the following entries:

Actual Cost of the New Engine ($5,000)
- Dr. Asset Cost.
- Cr. Cash/Debtor.

Make appropriate adjustments in the asset register and ensure that the new carrying amount of the asset comes to **41,894.41** (40,000 − 3,105.59 + 5,000).

DE-RECOGNITION

An item of property, plants, and equipment shall be derecognized when no further economic benefit is expected from its use, or when the asset is disposed of. This can also happen when any one of the following events occurs:

a) Sale or write-off.
b) Transfer to another class, for example from PPE to Inventory or Investment Property.

Note that depreciation ceases on de-recognition.

Gain on disposal shall not be recognized in the income statement, except for an entity that routinely sells such items as part of its normal business activities. However, such items of property, plant, and equipment must first be reclassified as held for sale (IFRS 5) before the actual sale.

Below is the summary of accounting entries for each case of a de-recognition event.

SALE

(a) Original Asset Cost
Dr. Asset Disposal.
Cr. Asset Cost.

(b) Accumulated Depreciation
Dr. Accumulated Depreciation.
Cr. Asset Disposal.

(c) Selling Price
Dr. Cashbook (or Debtor).
Cr. Asset Disposal.

(d) Profit or Loss

Profit
Dr. Asset Disposal.
Cr. Disposal Income or Other Comprehensive Income.

Loss
Dr. Disposal Expense (Profit or Loss).
Cr. Asset Disposal.

WRITE-OFF

One of the following two cases is likely to result from assets write-off:

(a) When the carrying amount is equal to zero.

This means the asset has served out its useful life. The following book entries apply:

Accumulated Depreciation
    Dr.   Accumulated Depreciation
    Cr.   Asset Cost

(b) When the carrying amount is not equal to zero
Here the asset is either damaged beyond restoration or is stolen while still in use. The following accounting entries apply:

Carrying Amount
    Dr. Asset Write-off
Accumulated Depreciation
    Dr. Accumulated Depreciation
Carrying Amount + Accumulated Depreciation
    Cr. Asset Cost

ALTERNATIVE METHOD
SALE

Original Asset Cost

Cr. Asset Cost Account

Accumulated Depreciation

Dr. Accumulated Depreciation Account

Selling Price

Dr. Cash (or Debtor) Account

Profit

Cr. Asset Disposal Account

OR

Loss

Dr. Asset Disposal Account

WRITE-OFF

Original Asset Cost

Cr. Asset Cost Account

Accumulated Depreciation

Dr. Accumulated Depreciation Account

Carrying Amount

Dr. Asset Disposal Account

TRANSFER

Assets are transferred at their carrying amount. The following accounting entries must accompany the asset transfer:

Carrying Amount
- Dr. Destination Asset Cost
- Cr. Source Asset Cost

Accumulated Depreciation
- Dr. Accumulated Depreciation
- Cr. Source Asset Cost

IMPLEMENTATION ISSUES

Let us now look at some of the key issues and tasks involved in the practical implementation of Fixed Assets accounting. They include the following:

1) Classifying the assets

2) Selecting accounting policies for each class of assets
3) Building the Fixed Assets Register
4) Applying the policies
5) Preparing the Disclosures

CLASSIFICATION

Organize the asset into distinct classes (Motor Vehicles, Plant and Machinery, Computer equipment, etc.) based on common policies, characteristics, and properties. This will enable consistent application of policies to each item within the class.

SELECTION OF ACCOUNTING POLICIES

For each class of asset, document accounting policies for the initial and subsequent measurements, as well as all other relevant information.

BUILDING THE FIXED ASSETS REGISTER

Your fixed assets register should capture all the relevant properties required to identify the asset, and parameters needed for subsequent measurements. Each item in the register must be assigned a unique code or ID, followed by a description. Some of the basic items you should have in the fixed asset register include:

1) Asset Code (unique for each item)
2) Description
3) Asset Class
4) Location
5) Date of Acquisition
6) Value Date (date actual use commences—if different from Date of Acquisition)
7) Initial Cost

8) Service Life
9) Residual Value
10) Depreciation Rate
11) Depreciation Method
12) Accumulated Depreciation
13) Accumulated Net Impairment Losses
14) Carrying Amount

All these are in addition to class-level policies and control parameters which apply to each item within the class.

APPLYING THE POLICIES

Consistently apply the selected measurement policies for each asset until the asset is de-recognized. For each measurement, update the fixed asset register as you make the book entries.

DISCLOSURES

Prepare your disclosures for presentation based on the requirements of the Standard. Take note of those disclosures that are expected to appear on the face of the financial statements, those that are expected on the fixed assets register, and those that are required as notes to the financial statements. Some of the standard items to be disclosed include
- a) **Measurement bases**
- b) **Depreciation method**
- c) **Useful life**
- d) **Depreciation rate**
- e) Gross **carrying amount**,
- f) **Accumulated depreciation**
- g) **Accumulated impairment losses**
- h) Assets classified as **held for sale**

SIMPLIFICATIONS FOR SMES

The following simplifications apply to small businesses under IFRS for SMEs:

1) Full IFRS requires an annual review of the **useful lives, residual values,** and **depreciation methods** of each item or a group of items. However, under IFRS for SMEs, the review is only necessary if there are indications of changes since the most recent annual reporting.
2) The revaluation model is not a mandatory option under IFRS for SMEs.
3) There is no provision for assets held for sale.

LEASES

Many of us are familiar with the word *Lease*, but the familiarity does not extend beyond its literal meaning. A lease is like a coin—one piece with two sides, with each side carrying a different inscription with different meanings. Understanding the various forms of leases is the first step toward a proper understanding of lease accounting.

DEFINITIONS & RECOGNITION

WHAT IS A LEASE?

IFRS defines a lease as **"an agreement whereby the lessor conveys to the lessee in return for a payment or series of payments the right to use an asset for an agreed period of time"**. This definition will provide the basis for deciding whether a transaction can be regarded as a lease or not—and not the legal contents of the agreement (substance over form).

INCEPTION OF A LEASE

This is the date of the lease agreement, or the date the parties involved in the lease agreement commit to the principle of the lease (whichever is earlier), while the ***commencement of the lease term*** is the date from which the lessee takes possession or begins to use the leased asset. Every lease provides for the **minimum lease**

payments, which are the amounts the lessee is expected to pay over the lease term.

RECOGNITION OF A LEASE

A lease is recognized by its substance and not by the legal form of the agreement. The fact that an agreement uses the word "lease" does not automatically make such a transaction a lease agreement. Every agreement should be carefully evaluated to see if it conforms to the formal definition of a lease as stated above.

CLASSIFICATION OF LEASES

Leases are classified as either **finance leases** or **operating leases**. A **finance lease** is defined as "a lease that transfers all the risks and rewards incidental to ownership" of the leased asset to the lessee with or without the transfer of title. Any lease other than a finance lease is to be classified as an **operating lease**. These two classifications are very important to the proper understanding of leases because each classification follows different accounting treatments.

The classification of a lease as either finance or operating and the determination of amounts to be recognized at the commencement of the lease term (for finance lease) is done at the **inception of the lease**.

LEASE INVOLVING LAND AND BUILDING

Under the provisions of the International Financial Reporting Standards (IFRS), it is possible to classify land with indefinite economic life as a finance lease even without the transfer of title to the lessee. Moreover, where a lease involves land and buildings, the portion that relates to land and the portion that relates to buildings must be classified separately. This, no doubt, could result in different classifications for land and building under the same agreement.

LEASE MEASUREMENTS FOR *LESSEES*

Let us now turn our attention to the issue of measurements of finance and operating leases for both the **lessors** and the **lessees**.

FINANCE LEASE

Under a finance lease, we must note that the lessee has acquired an asset, with the lease arrangement serving as an instrument for financing the acquisition of the asset. Thus, at the commencement of the lease term, the *lessee* shall recognize the lower of the **Fair Value** of the leased asset or the **Present Value** of the minimum lease payments (which comprises both the principal and finance charge) as asset and liability simultaneously. The discounting rate used in the calculation of the Present Value should be the same as the interest rate in the lease agreement. All initial direct costs attributable to negotiating and arranging the lease are capitalized along with the leased asset as part of the initial measurement.

Subsequently, the lease payments shall be recognized. The lease payments, which should be apportioned between the repayment of outstanding liability and the finance charge, shall be recognized on a constant periodic basis with the finance charge allocated to profit or loss for each period.

Note that a finance lease often gives rise to noncurrent assets, which must be accounted for as Property, Plant, and Equipment. The depreciation policy used should be consistent with that of the group to which the asset belongs. The asset is to be depreciated over the shorter of its **useful life** or the **lease term**, with the resulting depreciation expense allocated to profit or loss.

OPERATING LEASES

Under an operating lease, the lessee recognizes lease payments as an expense on a straight-line basis over the lease period (or term). Other than a straight line, any other basis that is more representative of the pattern of benefits the lessee derives from the leased assets can also be used. Lease expense, which excludes insurance and maintenance costs, is apportioned to profit or loss. The difference between the recognized lease expense and the actual payments made as of the reporting date is recognized as an **operating lease asset or liability** in the Statement of Financial Position.

It is necessary to take note of special incentives such as interest-free or rent-free periods provided by the *lessor*. These incentives do not imply zero charges for the period; they are to be added to the entire lease so that the overall effect will result in reduced payments over the entire lease period.

LEASE MEASUREMENTS FOR *LESSOR*

FINANCE LEASE MEASUREMENTS

Having transferred all the rewards and risks of ownership of the leased assets to the lessee, the lessor shall, at the commencement date, derecognize the leased asset and recognize a **receivable** equal to the **net investment in the lease**. **Initial direct costs** (costs attributable to negotiating and arranging the lease) are included in the finance lease receivable.

Subsequent measurement of finance lease income is based on a systematic pattern that depicts a constant periodic rate of returns on the leased asset over the lease term. **Lease receipts** (lessee's payments) are apportioned to the principal (leading to a reduction in the lessee's debt) and to (unearned) finance income for the period. For finance leases involving **manufacturer or dealer**

Lessors, the transaction is treated as outright sales, and this gives rise to the following income:

a) Initial recognition of **sales revenue** which is the minimum of either the fair value of the leased asset or the present value of minimum lease receipts based on the market rate of interest.
b) Subsequent periodic recognition of **finance income** over the lease term.

Initial direct costs incurred (such as administrative costs) for arranging the lease are recognized as expenses at the same time sales revenue is recognized. **Cost of sales** is the cost or carrying amount of the asset.

OPERATING LEASE MEASUREMENTS

In the case of an operating lease, ownership of the leased asset remains with the lessor and the asset continues to be accounted for as Property, Plant, and Equipment or as Intangible Assets.

The lessor shall recognize **lease income** from the operating lease on a straight-line basis over the lease term, or based on any other method that is more representative of the pattern of diminished benefit from the leased asset.

Costs incurred in the course of earning the lease income (including depreciation on the leased assets) are recognized as expenses. All initial direct costs incurred by the *lessors* are added to the carrying amount of the leased assets and recognized as expenses over the lease term on the same periodic pattern as the lease income.

The above pattern of income recognition also applies to manufacturer or dealer lessors. This is because an operating lease cannot be recognized as sales since it does not transfer the risks and rewards of the leased assets to the lessee.

SUMMARY OF ACCOUNTING ENTRIES FOR LEASES

FINANCE LEASE

LESSEE
Let us adopt the following notations:
Lease Amount (Present Value) — A
Lease Payment (Principal) — P
Interest Payment (Interest) — I

Associated Accounts
a) Lease Asset (NCA)
b) Lease Liability (AP)
c) Interest Expense (P or L)
d) Lease Payable Clearing Account (Liability)

Initial Measurement (Lessee Recognizes the Asset)
- Dr: Lease Asset Cost (A)
- Cr: Lease Liability (Lessor) (A)

Subsequent Measurement (Recognition of periodic Expense on Principal and Interest)
- Dr: Lease Liability (P)
- Dr: Interest Expense (I)
- Cr: Lease Payment Clearing A/C (P+I)

Cash Payment (Principal + Interest)
- Dr: Lease Payment Clearing A/C
- Cr: Cash Book

Note that cash payment based on agreed terms may or may not coincide with recognition of lease expense. The two transactions must be recognized separately.

LESSOR

Let us adopt the following notations:
Lease Amount (Net Investment)   A
Lease Receipt (Principal)   P
Interest Receivable (Interest)   I

Associated Accounts
a) Lease Receivable (Asset/Debtor)
b) Unearned Lease Income (Liability)
c) Lease Revenue (P or L)
d) Interest Income (P or L)
e) Lease Receivable Clearing Account (Asset)

Initial Measurement (Lessor recognizes Unearned Income)
  Dr: Lease Receivable (Lessee)   (A)
  Cr: Unearned Lease Income   (A)

Subsequent Measurement (Recognition of periodic Income from Principal and Interest)
  Cr: Lease Receivable   (P+I)
  Cr: Lease Revenue   (P)
  Cr: Lease Interest Income   (I)
  Dr: Unearned Lease Income   (P+I)
  Dr: Lease Receivable Clearing A/C   (P+I)

Cash Receipt (Principal + Interest)
  Dr: Cash Book
  Cr: Lease Receivable Clearing A/C

Note that the cash receipt, based on agreed terms, may or may not coincide with the recognition of lease income. The two transactions must be carried out separately.

De-recognition of Leased Assets

The lessor will have to de-recognize the leased asset since ownership has been fully transferred to the lessee. However, the accounting entries required for this depend on how the leased asset is classified in the book of the lessor. Detailed discussion on this can be found in my book, **MAKE IT REAL: IFRS ACCOUNTING FOR FINANCE AND REAL ESTATE**.

MANUFACTURER OR DEALER LESSORS

Initial Measurement (Sale of the Asset)

Dr:	Lease Receivable	(A+I)
Cr:	Sales Revenue	(A)
Cr:	Unearned Interest Income	(I)

Subsequent Measurement

Cr:	Lease Receivable	(P+I)
Cr:	Interest Income	(I)
Dr:	Unearned Interest Income	(I)
Dr:	Lease Receivable Clearing A/C	(P+I)

Receipt

Dr:	Cash Book	
Cr:	Lease Receivable Clearing A/C	

OPERATING LEASE

LESSEE

The Lessee recognizes the monthly rental expenses paid to the lessor:

Dr.	Rental Expense.	
Cr.	Cash/Lessor's Payable A/C.	

LESSOR
The leased asset belongs to the Lessor and is accounted for as Property, Plant, and Equipment (Chapter 10) or as Inventory. The Lessor recognizes monthly rental income as follows:

        Dr.   Cashbook/Lessee's Receivable A/C.
        Cr.   Rental Income.

FINANCIAL STATEMENTS AND SUNDRY REPORTS

One of the primary objectives of the IASB (International Accounting Standards Board) is to ensure uniformity and consistency in financial reporting. It is for this reason the body has prescribed a uniform reporting format for all entities. While the implementation of the various accounting policies may be considered an internal issue within each entity, financial statements must remain open for public scrutiny. It is the financial statements, which convey information about the performance and financial health of the entity to the world on. Business owners, regulators, investors, and the public need such information.

So far, we have been dealing with the first three methods of accounting, namely, Classification, Recognition, and Measurements. Now is the time to deal with the third component—Presentation.

No matter the neatness of your classification and the accuracy of your measurements, whatever you have inside your system remains internal to you or in a pure data format that may not make sense to everybody. People can only make sense of all the work you have put into keeping your books through the reports you present to them. It therefore means that any system that cannot produce accurate reports that conform to the prescribed standard is not good enough.

Presentation of Financial Statements is one of the Standards prescribed by the International Financial Reporting Standards

(IFRS). IFRS has prescribed the minimum information that should appear in each of these reports, as well as several other disclosures that must be prepared and presented along with the financial statements.

FINANCIAL STATEMENTS

A COMPLETE SET OF FINANCIAL STATEMENTS

A **complete set of financial statements** comprises the following:

a) **Statement of Financial Position** (formerly Balance Sheet – SMEs are allowed to retain the name Balance Sheet) at the end of the period.
b) **Statement of Comprehensive Income** (formerly Income Statement) for the period.
c) **Statement of Changes in Equity** for the period.
d) **Statement of Cash Flows** for the period.
e) **Notes** to the financial statements that contain accounting policies and other explanatory information.

Any related additional financial and non-financial information, such as financial review by management, explanation of the main features of the entity's financial performance and position, environmental reports, etc.

IDENTIFICATION AND PRESENTATION OF THE FINANCIAL STATEMENTS

An entity shall identify each financial statement and the notes with headings and sub-headings. In addition, an entity shall display the following information prominently, and repeat it when necessary:

a) The name of the reporting entity.
b) Whether the financial statements are of an individual entity or a group of entities.
c) The date of the end of the reporting period or the period covered by the set of financial statements.
d) The presentation currency.
e) The level of rounding used in presenting amounts in the financial statements.

This can be achieved by presenting appropriate headings for pages, statements, notes, columns, etc.

STATEMENT OF FINANCIAL POSITION

This was formerly called the **Balance Sheet**—SMEs are allowed to retain the name, Balance Sheet. As the name implies, the Statement of Financial Position presents the financial position of an entity (its assets, liabilities, and equities) as of any given date. Items on the statement of financial position are organized based on current/noncurrent assets and current/noncurrent liabilities by default. However, the liquidity-based approach, where items are arranged according to the order in which they are expected to be liquidated, can also be used if it will provide more clarity and reliability.

The minimum information required on the face of a Statement of Financial Position can be summarized and classified as follows:

Assets
a) Property, plant, and equipment (can be disaggregated into sub-classes based on IAS 16).
b) Investment property.
c) Intangible assets.
d) Financial Assets.
e) Investments.
f) Biological Assets.

g) Inventories (can be sub-classed according to IAS 2).
h) Receivables (disaggregated into customers' receivables, prepayments, and other receivables).
i) Deferred tax assets.
j) Cash and cash equivalents.
k) Assets held for sale (IFRS 5).

Liabilities
a) Trade and other payables
b) Provisions (sub-classed into various categories)
c) Financial liabilities.
d) Deferred tax liabilities.

Equity
a) Issued Capital and Reserves attributable to Owners
b) Other Reserves.
c) Non-controlling interests.

Line Items Disclosure or Notes

The following information must also appear either on the face of the **Statement of Financial Position** or in **notes**:

a) Nature and purpose of each Reserve.
b) Shareholders for dividends not formally approved for payment.
c) Amount of cumulative preference dividend not recognized.

STATEMENT OF COMPREHENSIVE INCOME (INCOME STATEMENT)

The **Statement of Comprehensive Income**, also known as the **Income Statement**, provides information about the performance of an entity over a given period. The minimum information to be presented on the face of the Statement of Comprehensive Income includes the following:

Revenue
a) Sale of Goods
b) Sale of Services
c) Interest Income
d) Royalties
e) Dividends
f) Other Income

Expense
a) Cost of Sales.
b) Administrative Cost.
c) Finance Cost.
d) Share of profits or losses of associates or joint ventures.
e) Tax Expense.
f) Profit or loss for the period attributable to non-controlling interest and owners of the parent.
g) Each component of Other Comprehensive Income, classified by nature
h) Total Comprehensive Income for the period attributable to non-controlling interest and owners of the parent.
i) Reclassification Adjustments recognized in profit or loss,
j) Other Expenses.

OTHER COMPREHENSIVE INCOME (OCI)

These are items of income and expenses not recognized in profit or loss as permitted by IFRS. They include the following:

a) Changes in revaluation surplus of fixed and intangible assets (IAS 16 & 38).
b) Additional gain or loss on defined benefit plans (IAS 19).

c) Gains or losses arising from translating the financial statements of foreign operations (IAS 21).
d) Gains or losses on re-measuring available-for-sale financial assets (IAS 39).
e) Cash flows from hedging instruments (IAS 39).

SMEs are exempted from presenting OCI unless there are items to present.

TOTAL COMPREHENSIVE INCOME

This is the Change in Equity resulting from transactions other than those changes resulting from transactions with owners in their capacity as owners of the business. This is computed as the **sum of Profit or Loss + Other Comprehensive Income**.

Line Items Disclosures or Notes

Additional information to be presented on the face of the statement of **Comprehensive Income** or **Notes** includes the following:

1. Analysis of expenses based on either nature or function.
2. If expenses are classified by function, disclosures of the following are required:
    a) Depreciation charges for tangible assets.
    b) Amortization charges for intangible assets.
    c) Employee benefits expense.
    d) Dividends recognized and the related amount per share.

STATEMENT OF CHANGES IN EQUITY

This is a statement of the increase or decrease in net assets or wealth. The minimum information required on the face of the Statement of Changes in Equity is as follows:

1) Total Comprehensive Income for the period showing separately the total amount attributable to owners of the parent and non-controlling interests.
2) The effects of retrospective application (e.g. changes in accounting policies) or restatements recognized (e.g. correction of errors) in accordance with IAS 8 on each of the components of equity.
3) Reconciliation between the carrying amount at the beginning and end of the period for each component of equity.

Line Items Disclosures or Notes

Additional information to be presented on the face of the statement of **Changes in Equity** or the **Notes** includes:

1) Capital transaction with owners and distributions to owners.
2) The amount of dividends recognized as distributions to owners during the period and the related per-share information.
3) Reconciliation of the balance of accumulated profit or loss at the beginning and end of the year.
4) Reconciliation of the carrying amount of each class of equity capital, share premium, and each reserve at the beginning and end of the period.

STATEMENT OF CASH FLOWS

The Statement of Cash Flows provides information that can be used to assess the viability (solvency and liquidity position) of an entity. Essentially, the cash flows show the sources of the cash inflow received by an entity during an accounting period and the purposes for which cash was used. See Chapter 13 for a full discussion on Cash Flows.

GENERAL DISCLOSURES REQUIREMENTS

Other additional disclosures that should accompany the financial statements as notes include the following:

1. **Capital Disclosures**
   Entities are required to define what they consider "capital", their objectives, policies, and processes for managing capital. They are also required to provide quantitative data about the capital.
2. A **summary of accounting policies**, and other **explanatory notes** (with cross-reference from the face of financial statements to the Notes) must be provided.
3. **Judgment made by management** in applying accounting policies that have the most significant effect on the amounts recognized in the financial statements.
4. **Estimation uncertainty**: Key assumptions about the future and other key sources of estimation uncertainty that have a significant risk of causing a material adjustment to the carrying amount of assets and liabilities within the next year.
5. **Other Disclosures** include the following:
   a) Domicile of the entity.

b) Legal form of the entity.
c) Country of incorporation.
d) Registered office, business address, or both.
e) Nature of operations, or principal activities, or both.
f) Name of the parent and ultimate parent.
g) The amount of dividends proposed or declared before the financial statements were authorized for issue, but not recognized as a distribution to owners during the period, and the related amount per share.
h) Amount of cumulative preference dividend not recognized.

CUSTOM FINANCIAL REPORTS

All the above requirements apply to general-purpose financial statements. However, many entities do require specialized and custom reports that are required for analyses and internal decision making. These general-purpose financial statements do not overwrite the need for such reports. Some of the special reports include:

1) Custom management report
2) Trial balance
3) Daybook or Journal
4) Ledgers
5) Invoices, Receipts
6) Vouchers
7) Bank Reconciliation report
8) Statements of accounts
9) Analyses of Income and Expenditure
10) VAT Analysis/Return

A good accounting system should be able to provide some of these reports as part of its standard offering. Some systems may even provide you with tools to script your reports.

STATEMENT OF CASH FLOWS

You have heard the statement "Cash is King." Yes, it is true. You have also heard that *Income is not equal to Cash*. This is also true—because some sales may have been on credit. You can fake sales, but you cannot forge cash. Cash is real and physical; it is either in your hands or in the bank. If you do not have cash your business will suffer and could die unless you get a blood transfusion—I mean cash transfusion. Now we can also add that Cash is the blood of your business—it supplies everything other organs of your business need to function effectively. And that is why I am devoting this chapter to studying its flow.

UNDERSTANDING CASH FLOWS

We have already discussed some of the important financial statements and sundry reports that should accompany every accounting system, including the Cash Flows Statement. But even the International Accounting Standards Board (IASB) has devoted one full standard to cash flows. We are also going to examine cash flows further in this chapter.

Most of us are quite familiar with the Balance Sheet and Income Statement; even the regulatory authorities seem to be more interested in these two. Balance Sheets and Income Statements have received so much attention for several reasons:

a) They have always been the classical parameters for evaluating the health of entities
b) CEOs (Chief Executive Officers) and CFOs (Chief Financial Officers) like them because they can easily be *loaded* to present a more brilliant picture of the company to investors and the public.
c) They are easy to prepare and quick to understand.
d) Not much has been said about Cash Flows because of the following factors:
e) They present hard facts about the true liquidity of the entity (many entities would not like to display such facts publicly).
f) They are not as easy to prepare and understand as the Balance Sheet and Income Statements.
g) Most CFOs see Cash Flow statements as a tool for financial management and control, and not accounting.

However, with the discovery of many high-profile financial improprieties due to manipulation of the figures (especially sales) by many reputable companies early this century, attention is gradually being shifted to cash flows as the parameter for measuring the true financial health of an entity. Cash, unlike the Income Statement and the Balance Sheet, is not easy to manipulate. A company with a rosy Balance Sheet and a hefty profit can still go kaput without cash. So really, Cash is King, as some would like to say.

To underscore the importance of Cash Flows, the **International Accounting Standards Board (IASB)** has assigned a separate Standard to it from the other two. It is the only financial statement that has been given this special treatment.

But what is Cash Flow?

Cash flow is simply the amount of cash flowing into and out of a business. Essentially, the cash flows show the sources of the cash inflow received by an entity during an accounting period and the purposes for which cash was used.

CLASSIFICATION OF CASH FLOW

Cash Flows are classified into the following categories:

CASH FROM OPERATING ACTIVITIES

These are the cash flows (in and out) used in the actual business operations of the entity. They include all payable and receivable transactions.

CASH FROM INVESTING ACTIVITIES

These are cash flows (in and out) resulting from investments and the purchase of assets, such as Property, Plant, and Equipment.

CASH FROM FINANCING ACTIVITIES

These are cash flows (in and out) from borrowings, loans, and transactions between the entity and its owners or shareholders, such as dividend payments, equity investments, etc.

Each category of cash flow tells a story—it tells where the cash is coming from and what the owners or operators of the business are doing with the cash. For example, if the cash from Operating Activities is very high, then the company is said to be doing well in its primary area of business; if the cash going into investing activities is too small, then it says something about the future of the business and intentions of the owners—perhaps they are using the business as a *cash cow*.

HOW TO CALCULATE CASH FLOW

As earlier mentioned, the process of calculating cash flows is not as straightforward as that of the Balance Sheet and the Income Statements. Here I will provide a simple guide for those who may want to carry out the exercise manually (as for me, I leave such tasks to my accounting software).

Let us look at the key parameters in the Cash Flows calculation:

NET PROFIT

Remember, profit is not equal to cash unless all the sales are paid for in cash—which is not always the case for most businesses. What we try to do in a cash flow statement is find and **take out the noncash portion of the transactions from net profit** for the reporting period. This is the **indirect method** of cash flow calculation.

DEPRECIATION EXPENSE

Remember also that **Depreciation Expense** is a noncash item that is included in the computation of profit, so this item will have to be added back to net profit. The same applies to any other noncash item such as foreign exchange gain or loss.

ASSET

Sales increase revenue and assets. However, when payment is not made in cash noncash assets are increased while cash is reduced. Thus, we can say that an **increase in noncash assets reduces cash**. Therefore, an increase in noncash assets will have to be subtracted from the Net Profit.

Note that when it comes to Property, Plant, and Equipment (Fixed Assets), you will have to use the original asset cost and not their Carrying (or Net Book) Values. So, if the asset has already been depreciated make sure you add back the depreciation to arrive at the original cost.

LIABILITY

Purchases or expenses have the following effects:

a) Increase either asset (for capital expense) or overhead expense
b) Reduce liability and increase cash (if the items are not paid for in cash) or reduce cash and increase liability (if paid for in cash).

Thus, we can say that an **increase in liability leads to an increase in cash at hand** (because you are not using available cash to pay for the item). Therefore, we must add an increase in assets to Net Profit. If we then use the following notations:

nP = Net Profit
Dp = Depreciation
ΔA = Increase in Noncash Asset
ΔL = Increase in Liability

Then our formula for Cash Flow (CF) for any given period becomes

$CF = nP + Dp - \Delta A + \Delta L$

The data you need for this computation will come from the following sources:

a) Balance Sheet
b) Income Statement

Make sure you get these two reports correct and ready before you begin your cash flow calculations.

As I mentioned earlier, I do not compute Cash Flow manually; my accounting software does it for me, and I believe any good accounting software should be able to generate statements of Cash Flow from underlying data. But there is nothing wrong with exercising your brain. And there is beauty and satisfaction in getting the numbers done on your own.

DISCLOSURE REQUIREMENTS

Now let us turn our attention to IFRS disclosure requirements for the Statement of Cash Flows. The following specific requirements apply to cash flow:

1) Components of cash and cash equivalents in the statement of cash flows and reconciliation with the equivalent items in the statement of financial position.
2) Details about noncash investing and financing transactions (for example, conversion of debt to equity).
3) Amount of cash and cash equivalents held by the entity that are not available for use by the group.

If your Statement of Cash Flows is properly structured, items 1 and 2 should automatically appear on the face of your report. However, item 3 may not necessarily apply to SMEs.

14

CLOSING THE BOOKS

Accounting periods are delineated in months and quarters, and one accounting (or financial) year is made up of twelve months or four quarters. Accounting year can start from any month and end at any month, although most entities prefer the January—December range. No law governs the choice of accounting period. However, some national jurisdictions may prescribe a uniform accounting period for certain categories of businesses.

For regulatory purposes, all the financial statements and disclosure requirements discussed in the previous chapter apply to year-end reporting. Any report that covers less than one financial year is considered an interim report—the most common being quarterly financial statements. Entities must wait till the end of the year after all the entries and adjustments have been made before releasing their financial reports and then closing the book.

Apart from the financial statements, something very fundamental, with a tremendous impact on the financial data, happens at the end of every accounting year, when the books are formally closed.

CLOSING AND OPENING BALANCES

Closing the current year's account to start a new accounting year is a standard ritual that takes place before the beginning of every new accounting year. With your daily postings in order and your accounts balanced, you have nothing to worry about at the end of the year. However, your auditor may request some adjustment entries after auditing your accounts.

At the end of every accounting year, all the books must be closed for a new accounting year to commence. Closing the books involves computing the **closing balance** for each account for the period just ended and using the same figures as the **opening balance** for the new accounting year about to commence.

If you have not been depreciating your noncurrent (fixed) assets monthly, this is the right time to do that for the whole year. What that means is, that you will have to compute the depreciation on all your noncurrent assets using applicable depreciation rates, and update your book with the following journal entries:

      Dr.   Depreciation Expense (Profit or Loss)
      Cr.   Accumulated Depreciation

Generally, the following rules should be observed when closing your accounts for the year:

Assets, Liabilities, Capital/Equity Accounts

These are accounts referred to as *Balance Sheet items* or *non-Profit or Loss accounts*. The closing balance for each account under these categories should be transferred to the new accounting period as the opening balance.

Profit or Loss Accounts

Compute the net profit for the period. If the trading activities for the period result in a profit, then credit the **Retained Earnings** account with the profit, otherwise debit the account.

All the **Profit or Loss** (Income and Expense) accounts should start with zero opening balance in the new accounting year.

Note

a) Before closing your books, make sure all the entries for the period you want to close have been made, and all corrections and adjustments pertaining to that period carried out.
b) If you are using multiple currencies in recording your transactions, there may be a need to compute exchange rate differences for the foreign currencies, based on your **closing rates**. This is the cumulative difference between the spot rates used in recording transactions throughout the period and the closing rate you specify at the end of the period. This difference should be posted to the **Exchange Rates Translation** account under Equity.

Most accounting software provides tools designed to enable you to carry out all these operations automatically with ease.

ACCOUNTING AND THE INFORMATION SYSTEM IMPERATIVE

Accounting may have started several centuries ago but there is no reason why it should remain frozen in the past. The current disruptions which have taken many industries and professions by storm have already started taking their toll on accounting, but some people are trying to fight back. It is a battle they are bound to lose! This is not only the information age—it is also the knowledge age. The rigor and drudgery of accounting which have scared so many away for so long need to be eliminated because we all need accounting. This can only be achieved through the diligent application of smart information system solutions.

I did not write this book because I want to turn you into an accountant—I wrote it, primarily, because I want you to understand and appreciate what accounting is all about, and to know the practical relevance of the numbers on the financial statements. Beyond that, I want you to be able to roll up your sleeves and get your hands dirty doing the numbers if the need ever arises. This book is meant to help you achieve all that.

But let me make this point clear: most of the issues I have discussed in this book cannot be realized without the use of accounting software. Accounting software will not only lighten the burden of accounting but will also make it easy for you to implement accounting policies faster, cheaper, and more accurately.

There are people out there who go about encouraging small business owners to use spreadsheets or even pen and paper to record their financial transactions and then wait for the 'expert' to come and organize things properly. If you do not know what that means, let me tell you now: it is like being asked to write your scripts with pen and paper and then wait for a typist to come and type them for you using an IBM typewriter, even when you can afford a computer with a word processor. These people are not helping you—they are helping themselves at your expense. Accounting software will do the job cheaper, neater, and faster.

I am not saying you will no longer require the services of experts. Surely, you will need experts to advise and assist you in many areas of your business—including financial management. But having an 'expert' to do bookkeeping for you should, certainly, not be one of them.

THE INFORMATION SYSTEM SOLUTION IMPERATIVE

For us to clearly understand the expected role of information technology in solving modern accounting problems, let us examine the primary tasks and challenges involved in accounting.

THE PRIMARY TASKS

The primary tasks involved in accounting include the following, amongst others:

- a) Classification.
- b) Measurements.
- c) Presentation and Disclosures.

Classification

Asset, liability, revenue, and expenditure must be classified based strictly on the standard definition and recognition requirements. There is no room for arbitrary classification—everything must be placed in the correct group and order. The chart of accounts provides both the structural template and the physical store for your classification. The accuracy of your measurements and reports depends on this table as everything in the General Ledger must have its root in the chart of accounts. This dynamic table is better managed more accurately and effectively with software, even if your chart of accounts is only one page.

Measurements

It is very easy to determine your initial measurement based on the initial acquisition cost or fair value, but when it comes to subsequent measurements things could get a little bit messy. Think of depreciation of fixed assets, amortization of loans, etc. Surely, you are by far better off with an automated system that computes everything and makes the required entries, with little or no human intervention. Manual handling is slow, tedious, and prone to error.

Presentation and Disclosures

What we have listed so far can be regarded as behind-the-scene operations. What the outside world wants to see are the reports—financial statements, along with all the required disclosures. No matter what you have put in place, if you cannot produce financial statements then the job is not yet completed. But how and when do we have to produce reports? Do we have to wait for some 'expert' to come and organize things for us at the end of every month or year?

In a world where decisions are taken at the 'speed of light,' you will be putting yourself at a great disadvantage if you cannot tap into your system for relevant information anywhere anytime. This is one area where accounting software is indispensable: The production and presentation of real-time and accurate reports with maximum ease!

Closing and Opening Balances

We have already seen the various activities which take place at the end of every accounting year. You must close your books for the previous year and move the balances to the new accounting year for all the non-Profit or Loss accounts; you must compute your profit for the outgoing year and move the balance to retained earnings.... It sounds quite simple, but it can be very tedious and messy. These are some of the troubles you don't have to go through if you put accounting software in place.

There are many other things accounting software can help you do, beyond the ones I have highlighted here. But let these be the basic minimum of what you should expect from any accounting software.

ACCOUNTING SOFTWARE SOLUTION

Software is a great business tool and one investment you should not treat with levity. Even the data you generate is an asset that could form the raw materials for knowledge-based systems, such as data warehouses and data mining. The benefits of using accounting software outstrip whatever savings one may expect from a manual system, even if you are running a coffee shop. Shop for good accounting software and invest your time in learning how to use it productively. The solution provided by accounting software is cheaper, neater, faster, more accurate, and more reliable than any manual method, both in the short and the long term.

In Nigeria, this book comes with a free copy of the Basic Edition of **ABC Financial and Business Toolkit**—a simple accounting tool packaged as part of a project by Spectra Business Intelligence Limited to provide financial education and tools for small businesses. Buying a copy of this book entitles you to a free copy of the software. However, if your business requires something more than what the free Basic Edition can handle, you can upgrade to either the Standard or Professional Edition.

But remember, accounting software is not a *plug-and-play* device like your cell phone or DVD. You will have to put in some effort to learn and understand how to use it, no matter how simple it might appear. However, by reading and understanding this book you are already halfway through with the task of properly managing your finances. Now, you can go ahead and take your business to a new level.

www.ingramcontent.com/pod-product-compliance
Lightning Source LLC
Chambersburg PA
CBHW071923210526
45479CB00002B/534